鳥山　明

It feels like things have gotten even more hectic since the year started. In addition to **Dragon Ball**, I have some work I'm doing for a video game, some work for **V Jump**, and the work I'm doing with my friend designing model kits. And then, in whatever spare time I have left, I have to think up dozens of design plans for my company, Bird Studio. Just as I'm writhing in agony, my dog gets sick, and I've had to find time for trips to the vet. (She's fine now.) I want time to goof off!

–Akira Toriyama, 1994

Widely known all over the world for his playful, innovative storytelling and humorous, distinctive art style, **Dragon Ball** creator Akira Toriyama is also known in his native Japan for the wildly popular **Dr. Slump**, his previous manga series about the adventures of a mad scientist and his android "daughter." His hit series **Dragon Ball** ran from 1984 to 1995 in Shueisha's **Weekly Shonen Jump** magazine. He is also known for his design work on video games such as **Dragon Warrior**, **Chrono Trigger** and **Tobal No. 1**. His recent manga works include **Cowa!**, **Kajika**, **Sand Land**, **Neko Majin**, and a children's book, **Toccio the Angel**. He lives with his family in Japan.

DRAGON BALL Z VOL.22
SHONEN JUMP Manga Edition

STORY AND ART BY
AKIRA TORIYAMA

English Adaptation/Gerard Jones
Translation/Lillian Olsen
Touch-up Art & Lettering/Wayne Truman
Design/Sean Lee
Editor/Jason Thompson

In the original Japanese edition, DRAGON BALL and DRAGON BALL Z are known collectively as the 42-volume series DRAGON BALL. The English DRAGON BALL Z was originally volumes 17–42 of the Japanese DRAGON BALL.

Printed in the U.S.A.

Published by VIZ Media, LLC
P.O. Box 77010
San Francisco, CA 94107

10
First printing, September 2005
Tenth printing, April 2018

SHONEN JUMP MANGA

DRAGON BALL Z

Vol. 22

DB: 38 of 42

STORY AND ART BY
AKIRA TORIYAMA

THE MAIN CHARACTERS

Piccolo
An alien from planet Namek.
Son Goku
Gohan's father, he is one of the last of the Saiyans, a super-strong alien race.
Son Gohan
A teenage half-Saiyan. Currently in disguise as the "Great Saiyaman."
#18
A powerful and temperamental cyborg.
Vegeta
The prince of the Saiyans, he is Goku's archrival.
Kuririn
oku's former martial arts classmate. He is married to #18.
Trunks
The half-Saiyan son of Vegeta and Bulma (not pictured).
Son Goten
Goku's second half-Saiyan son (after Gohan).

Son Goku was Earth's greatest hero, and the Dragon Balls, which can grant any wish, were Earth's greatest treasure. After many adventures, Goku finally died saving the world from the monstrous Cell, but he left behind two sons, Gohan and Goten. When a great martial arts tournament was announced, Goku's old friends gathered to participate...and even Goku came down from heaven to join in on the action! But before the tournament could really get started, it was interrupted by the arrival of two otherworldly visitors: Kaiô-shin, the mighty "lord of lords," and his right-hand man, Kibito. Kaiô-shin had come to earth to track down the diabolical wizard, Bobbidi...and he needs our heroes' help!

DRAGON BALL Z 22

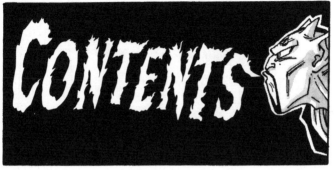

CONTENTS

DRAGON BALL

ドラゴン
ボール

DBZ:252 •
Bobbidi the Warlock

SO BASICALLY...
WE HAVE TO STOP THEM FROM RESURRECTING THIS BOO.
PRECISELY.
WHICH MEANS DEFEATING BOBBIDI FIRST.
IS HE TOUGH?
NOT PHYSICALLY... BUT HE USES MAGIC. HIS FATHER BIBBIDI WAS THE SAME.
WARLOCKS TAKE ADVANTAGE OF THE EVIL WITHIN PEOPLE AND TAKE CONTROL OF THEM, AS HE DID WITH SPOPOVICH AND YAMU.
LET'S JUST HOPE HE DOESN'T HAVE ANYONE FORMIDABLE ON HIS SIDE.

READ THIS WAY

SO WHY WERE SPOPOVICH AND YAMU AT THE TOURNAMENT?
...AND WHAT DID THEY DO TO ME?
BOO HAS BEEN SEALED AWAY FOR A LONG TIME. TO RESURRECT HIM, BOBBODI NEEDS A TREMENDOUS AMOUNT OF PURE ENERGY.
HE KNEW HE COULD TAP SUCH ENERGY QUICKLY AT THE TOURNAMENT. YOU WERE A PERFECT SOURCE WHEN YOU TURNED SUPER SAIYAN...
...JUST AS WE ANTICIPATED.
...
BUT WE NEEDED TO FIND HIS HIDEOUT. BOO'S SHELL WASN'T WHERE IT WAS LEFT BEFORE.
THAT'S WHY WE HAD TO FOLLOW SPOPOVICH AND YAMU.

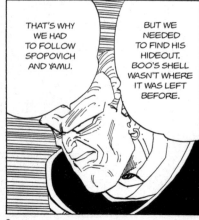

WHY'D YOU LEAVE THIS DJINN LYING AROUND IF YOU KNEW WHAT IT COULD DO?!

AND WE THOUGHT IT WOULD BE SAFE, SINCE THE SHELL WAS AT A PLACE INACCESSIBLE TO HUMANS.

WE HAD NO CHOICE. WE DIDN'T KNOW WHAT COULD BREAK THE SEAL.

WE'VE GOT TO GO FASTER!

WE'LL NEVER CATCH UP AT THIS SPEED!

I CAN'T EVEN KEEP MY EYES OPEN!

THIS IS AS FAST AS I CAN GO...!

READ THIS WAY

VIDEL, YOU SHOULD TURN BACK.
THIS SOUNDS WAY RISKIER THAN I THOUGHT.
...I GUESS I SHOULD... I CAN'T POSSIBLY BE ANY HELP TO YOU...
...BUT I HATE TO ADMIT IT.
THANKS.
IF YOU FIND GOTEN OR MY MOM AT THE TOURNAMENT, LET 'EM KNOW ABOUT THIS, OK?
SURE. SAY... YOU **WERE** THE GOLDEN WARRIOR, WEREN'T YOU?
YOUR FRIENDS WERE AT THE BATTLE WITH CELL SEVEN YEARS AGO...
AND YOU WERE THE LITTLE KID WITH 'EM, HUH?
...YEAH.
...
...YEAH.
THEN MY DAD WASN'T THE ONE WHO KILLED CELL.
IT WAS YOU GUYS, WASN'T IT?!
I'M SORRY I LIED... I DIDN'T WANT ANYONE TO KNOW...

I ALWAYS THOUGHT THERE WAS SOMETHING FISHY ABOUT THAT STORY.
AT LEAST I KNOW THE TRUTH!
...I KNEW IT... YOU DON'T HAVE TO HAVE TO PROTECT MY DAD.
W-WELL...
YOU GOT IT !!
GIVE THAT BOBBIDI WHAT HE'S ASKIN' FOR!!
GOOD LUCK, GOHAN !
ARE YOU DONE? WE'VE GOT TO CATCH UP TO THE REST.
SORRY FOR THE DELAY!
YEAH !
OK !!
I'LL BE WAITING AT THE TOURNAMENT!!

READ THIS WAY

VINN
VINN
KIIIIIN
...TH- THEY'RE SO FAST...!
...
BE CAREFUL, GOHAN.
IF YOU COME BACK SAFE...I'M GONNA ASK YOU OUT!
FIGHT

READ THIS WAY
THEY'RE MAKING THEIR DESCENT... !
!
!!
WEIRD... WE CHECKED THIS AREA BEFORE...
EVERY-ONE SUPPRESS YOUR CHI!

HYOOOO---
I SEE SOMEBODY! IS THAT BOBBIDI?
NO.
...IS IT JUST ME, OR DOES IT LOOK WEIRD OVER THERE...? LIKE THEY DUG UP THE GROUND...?

READ THIS WAY

OF COURSE! HIS SHIP WAS HIDDEN UNDER-GROUND!
THAT'S WHY WE NEVER FOUND IT!
WHICH MEANS HE KNOWS WE'RE HERE ON EARTH. OTHERWISE...
...WHY BOTHER HIDING HIS SHIP?
WE SHOULD MAKE OUR MOVE BEFORE THEY CAN USE GOHAN'S ENERGY AND RESURRECT BOO!!

NO. THEY'LL COME OUTSIDE TO RESURRECT BOO SO THEY DON'T DESTROY THE SHIP.
WE CAN MAKE OUR MOVE THEN. LET'S WAIT AND SEE...
...
WRRR
SOME-ONE'S COMING OUT !!

DBZ:253 • The Evil Masters

DABRA!! BOBBIDI EVEN HAS THE KING OF THE DEMON PLANE UNDER HIS COMMAND!!
THAT'S TROUBLE...
HE'S THE LAST ONE I EXPECTED TO SEE...

READ THIS WAY

WHICH ONE?! THE BIG GUY?
YES.
IS HE THAT TOUGH...?
YOU DON'T BECOME KING OF THE DEMONS THROUGH NICENESS.
YOU MAY BE THE STRONGEST IN THIS WORLD, BUT IN THE REALM OF EVIL—HE WINS EVERY CONTEST!
...
TH-THE "DEMON PLANE"...? THERE'S A WHOLE 'NOTHER WORLD OF EVIL?
I REALLY, REALLY DON'T LIKE THE SOUND OF THAT...
SO THAT MEANS...
THE LITTLE GUY IS BOBBIDI?

HARD TO BELIEVE HE'S THE ONE...
INDEED.
...TURNED EVEN DABRA INTO HIS MINION.
DON'T LET HIS PHYSICAL WEAKNESS FOOL YOU. AFTER ALL, HIS MAGIC...
DABRA IS AN IDEAL CANDI-DATE.
NO. HE MANIPULATES THE EVIL AND GREED ALREADY LURKING IN ONE'S SOUL.
HIS MAGIC CAN OVERPOWER SUCH A FOE AS THAT?
THAT'S WHY YOU CAN'T HAVE ANY EVIL IN YOUR SOULS IF YOU'RE GOING TO FIGHT HIM.
THAT'S WHAT MAKES BOBBIDI'S MAGIC SO DANGEROUS. SO MANY POWERFUL BEINGS UNDER HIS SWAY.

READ THIS WAY

WE HADN'T COUNTED ON DABRA BEING HERE.
THIS MAKES THINGS VERY DIFFICULT.
YOU DON'T THINK WE CAN BEAT HIM?
...
HMPH. AND THE WORLD'LL END IF BOO'S RESURRECTED?
WELL, FORGET THAT. I'M NOT LOSING TO THEM.
KURIRIN, YOU SHOULD GO BACK. IT'S TOO DANGEROUS.
M-MAYBE I SHOULD... HA HA...
I M-M-MEAN IF I WON'T B-B-BE ANY USE...

AH, YOU FILLED IT WITH ENERGY! GOOD JOB! NOW WE ARE THAT MUCH CLOSER TO BOO'S RESURRECTION!
THANK YOU, SIR!!
IT WAS NOTHIN' FOR US!!
HEH
AND NOW... I DON'T NEED YOU ANYMORE.
HUH ?
KRAK

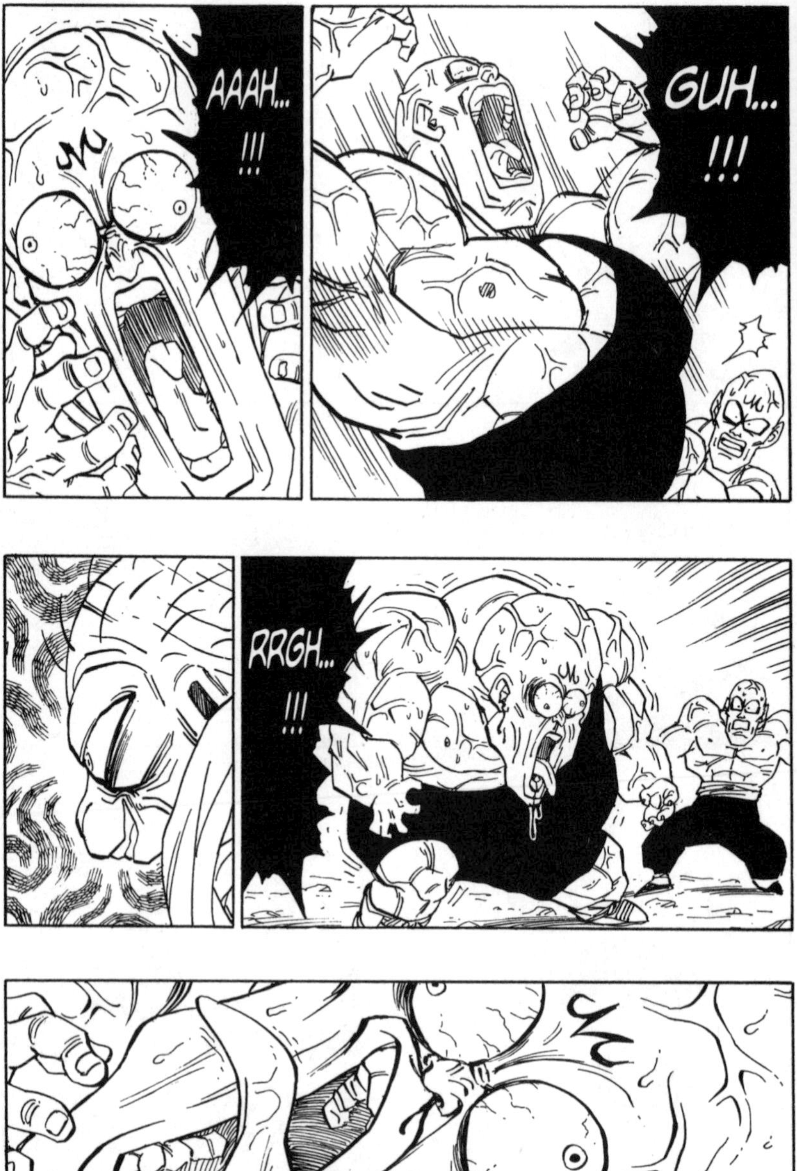
GUH...
!!!
AAAH...
!!!
RRGH...
!!!

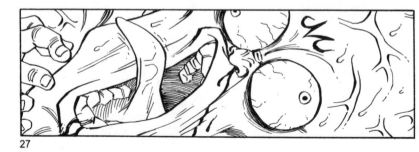

!!
BOOM
NUHHHH...
!!
OH...
!!
AAA
!!!!
"BOOM." WHAT A LOVELY SOUND!

READ THIS WAY

WOULD YOU LIKE TO GIVE IT A TRY, POCUS?
OH, YES !!
FSH
DM

NICE SHOT!

BOOM

HOW COULD THEY...?!

THEY... KILLED THEM...

AS I EXPECTED, THEY'VE BROUGHT US MORE ENERGY... ALONG WITH THE LORD OF LORDS...MY FATHER'S MURDERER.

YES?

NOW, DABRA...

READ THIS WAY

THEY THINK THEY'RE HIDDEN... I COUNT SEVEN IN ALL. WE CAN'T USE ENERGY FROM THE LORD OR KIBITO, BUT... THREE OF THEM HAVE GREAT POTENTIAL.
YEAH...THEY MIGHT GIVE US ALL THE ENERGY WE NEED!
HEE HEE! I DIDN'T THINK THE RESURRECTION WOULD COME THIS SOON!
OUR BEST BET IS TO LURE THEM INSIDE THE SHIP AND THEN SUCK THEIR ENERGY.
THE LORD OF LORDS WON'T LET THEM GO.
KILL THE RIFFRAFF AND GET BACK IN THE SHIP. THE OTHER THREE'LL GET MAD AND COME AFTER YOU.
OHO!
JUST DON'T KILL THE LORD OF LORDS.
I'LL DEAL WITH HIM MYSELF. SLOWLY.

I'LL MAKE SURE YOU HAVE YOUR FUN.
GOOD ENOUGH, BOBBIDI.
COME INSIDE. I'LL LET YOU HANDLE STAGE ONE.
DABRA WILL DO FINE BY HIMSELF.
MASTER BOBBIDI...?
Y-YES-SIR!!
LET'S GO!
NOW THEN...
THEN IT'S ALL YOURS.
THANK YOU!

READ THIS WAY

HUH? THEY'RE ALL GOING IN EXCEPT DABRA...?
WHAT... ?
HEH HEH
THEY KNOW WE'RE HERE !!!!
VZZ

NEXT: Nothing Ventured...

DBZ:254 • The Descent

BM
TOOM

KIBITO !!!!
SHOOT... !!!!
PTUI PTUI

READ THIS WAY

LOOK OUT!!!! IF HIS SALIVA TOUCHES YOU—!!!!
WHAT ?!
PECH
!!
EH ?!
PECH
ACK !!!
NH... GHH... !!!
OH NO !!!!

KURIRIN!! PICCOLO !!
WHAT'S WRONG ?!
AHA HA HA !!!
DON'T TOUCH THEM !!!
ARH... !!
THEY'VE BEEN TURNED TO STONE !!
IF YOU BREAK THEM— THEY'LL NEVER TURN BACK !!

READ THIS WAY

NEVER TURN BACK IF...?
THEN THERE'S STILL A WAY TO GET THEM BACK ?!
ONE WAY.
DABRA WILL HAVE TO DIE.
IS THAT ALL ?!
THAT'S EASY !!
WHAT ?!
YOU'D BETTER RUN HOME !!
NO ONE CAN DEFY MASTER BOBBIDI !!

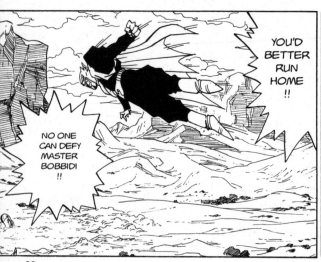

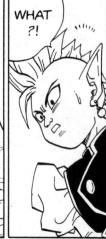

DAD, LET'S GO !!!
WE *ARE* GOING AFTER HIM, RIGHT ?!
WE'VE GOT TO SAVE KURIRIN AND PICCOLO !!
WHAT ELSE ?!
COME ON !!
WAIT!! WE MUSTN'T FALL FOR THEIR TRAP!!
THEY *WANT* US INSIDE THEIR SHIP!! THAT'S WHY THEY DID NOTHING TO YOU THREE!
B-BM
HEY !!!
SORRY. I'M NOT MADE FOR STANDING AROUND.

READ THIS WAY
BM
FSH
HEH
...IDIOTS... !!
BM
YOU...

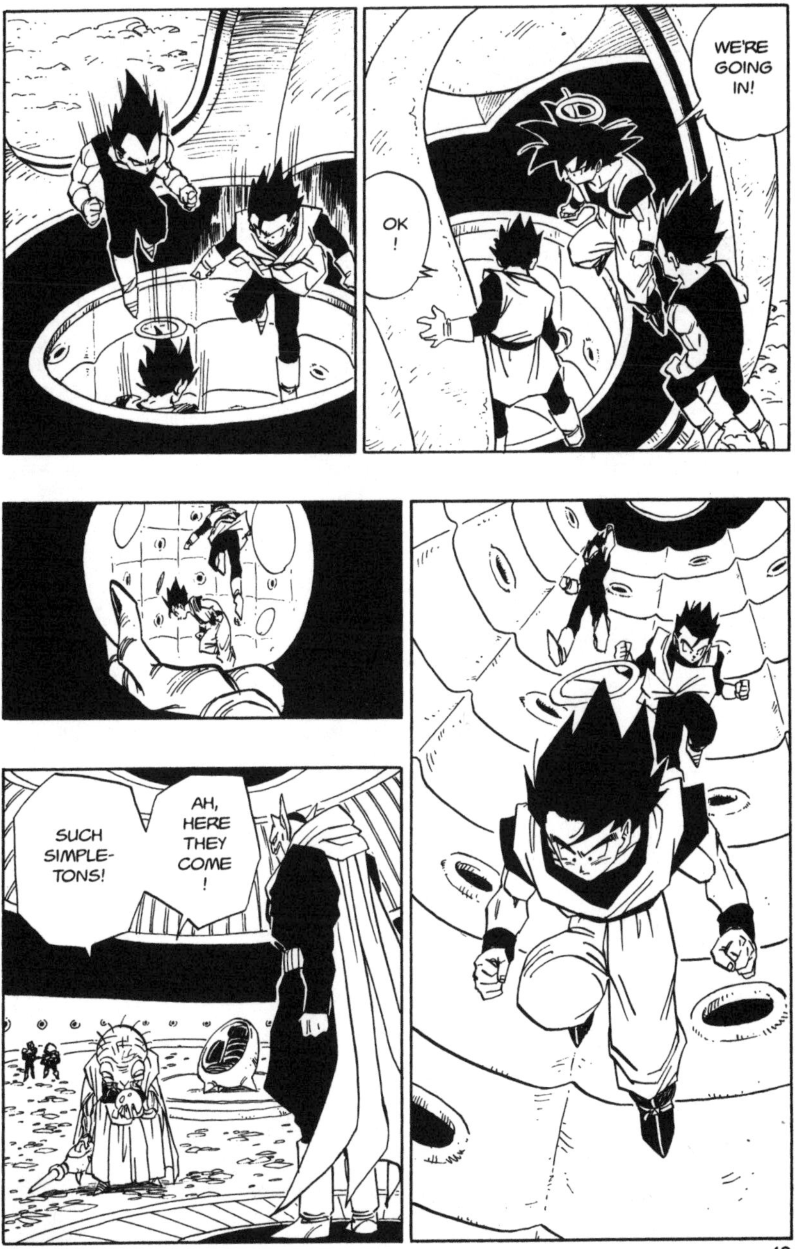

OK
!

WE'RE
GOING
IN!

SUCH
SIMPLE-
TONS!

AH,
HERE
THEY
COME
!

READ THIS WAY

T.T.TM
WHERE ARE WE?!
AN EMPTY ROOM...?
THERE'S A DOOR OVER THERE!
LET'S BREAK IT DOWN!
HUH?!
TM
SO YOU DID COME!
I CAN'T ABANDON YOU TO YOUR OWN IDIOCY!

WE'LL DESTROY THIS THING IF WE HAVE TO!

FEH!

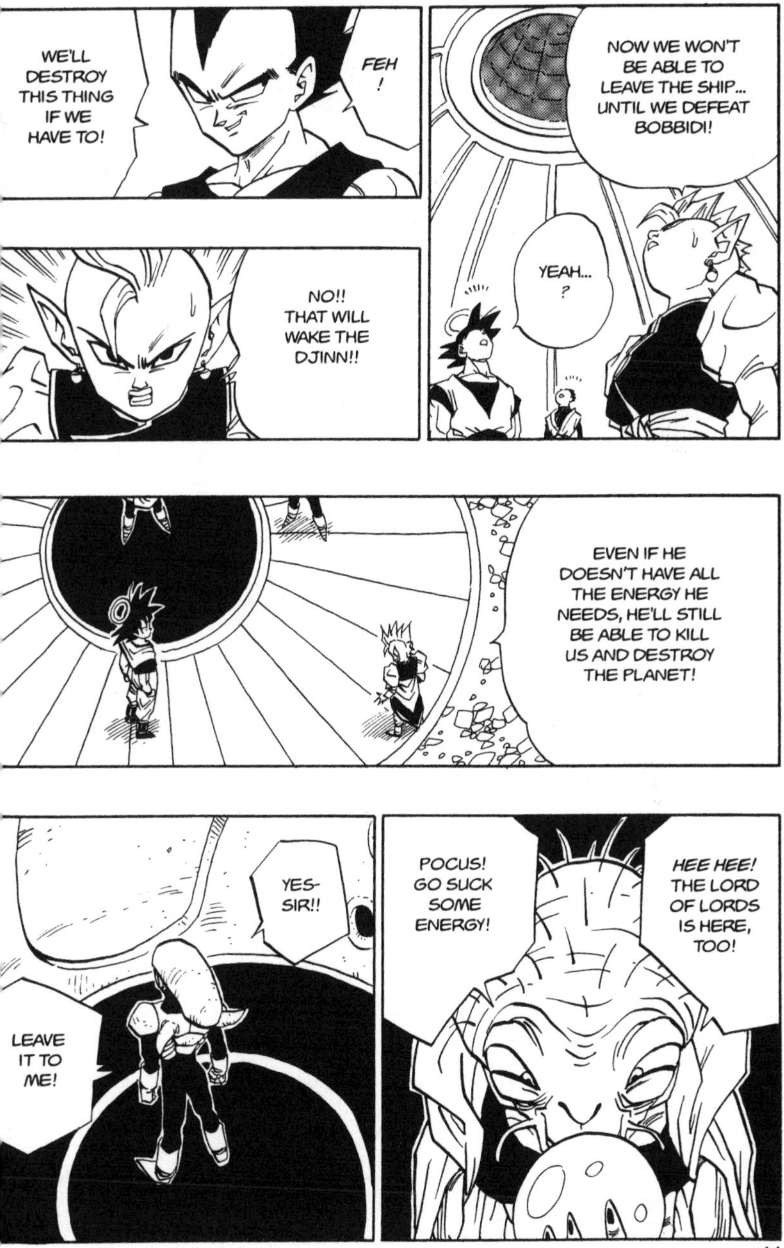

NOW WE WON'T BE ABLE TO LEAVE THE SHIP... UNTIL WE DEFEAT BOBBIDI!

YEAH...?

NO!! THAT WILL WAKE THE DJINN!!

EVEN IF HE DOESN'T HAVE ALL THE ENERGY HE NEEDS, HE'LL STILL BE ABLE TO KILL US AND DESTROY THE PLANET!

YES-SIR!!

POCUS! GO SUCK SOME ENERGY!

LEAVE IT TO ME!

HEE HEE! THE LORD OF LORDS IS HERE, TOO!

READ THIS WAY

WRR
MASTER BOBBIDI IS ON THE BOTTOM FLOOR.
HOW-EVER...
YOU CAN'T GO ANY FUR-THER...
UNTIL YOU DEFEAT ME!
YOU'VE REACHED THE END OF THE LINE!
HEH HEH HEH...
SORRY.
I DISAGREE.

NEXT: The Game

DBZ:255 • Stage One: Pocus

READ THIS WAY

THIS MUCH ENERGY IN ONE SHOT...?!
THAT'S ALMOST HALF WHAT WE NEED!!
WHAT ?!
DID THEY TAP HUNDREDS OF PEOPLE ?!
THEY DIDN'T SAY.
TSK.
I WOULDN'T HAVE KILLED THEM IF I'D KNOWN THEY COULD GET SO MUCH SO QUICKLY.
DON'T WORRY. THE ENERGY OF THOSE THREE IN STAGE ONE WILL PROBABLY FILL IT ALL THE WAY.
BOO WILL BE RESUR-RECTED BEFORE THE DAY IS OUT.

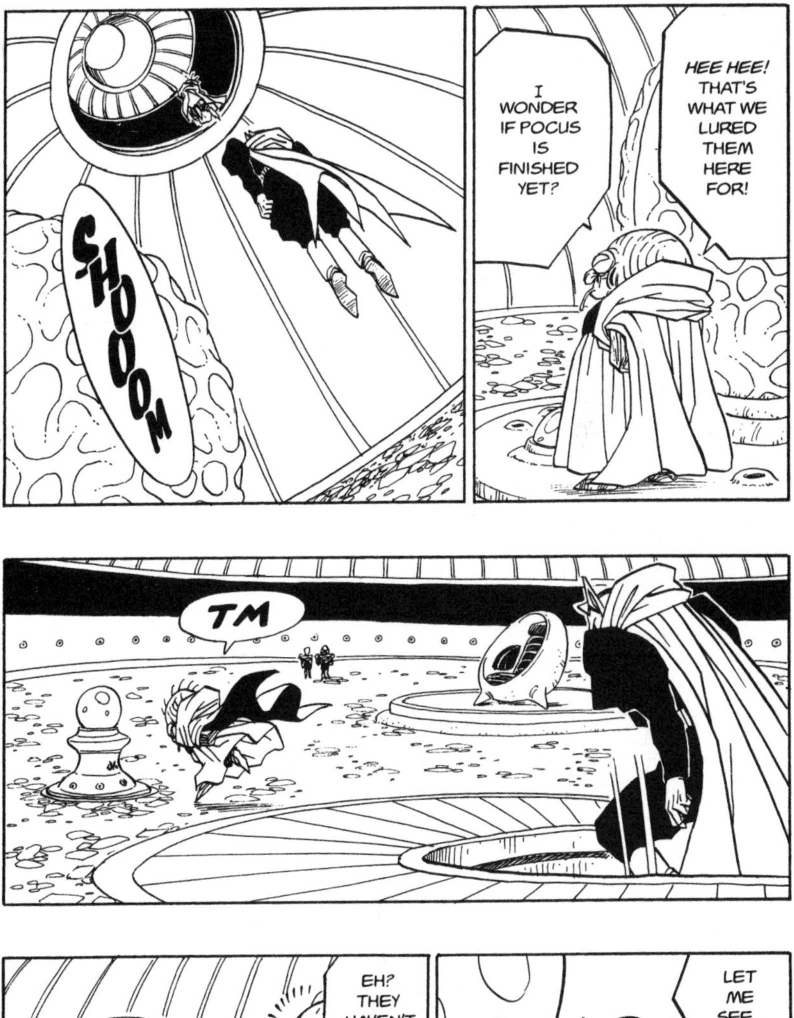
SHOOOM
I WONDER IF POCUS IS FINISHED YET?
HEE HEE! THAT'S WHAT WE LURED THEM HERE FOR!
TM
EH? THEY HAVEN'T EVEN STARTED ?!
LET ME SEE...

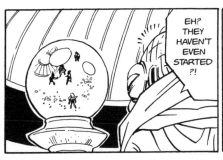

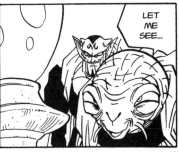

READ THIS WAY

...
ONE MORE TIME!
...
ONE MORE TIME!
AWW, RATS!
...WH-WHAT ARE THEY DOING...?
OK. ME FIRST.
B-BY YOURSELF?!
YOU THINK I CAN'T HANDLE IT?
HA! MASTER BOBBIDI TOLD ME TO BE CAREFUL... BUT THEY'RE FOOLS!

EASY, EASY. VEGETA'S GOT HIM.
DON'T UNDER-ESTIMATE THEM! THE WARRIORS BOBBIDI HAS COLLECTED ARE—
BOBBIDI'S THE FOOL. HE SHOULD KNOW NOT TO PICK A FIGHT WITHOUT DOING HIS RESEARCH!
HE'S JUST TAKEN ON THE STRONGEST BEINGS IN EXISTENCE!
STRONGEST IN...? *HA HA HA!!* YOU'RE INSANE!
HA! THERE'S NO ESCAPE NOW!
THE DAMAGE YOU SUFFER WILL BE CONVERTED TO ENERGY...
WHICH WILL BE CHANNELED INTO MASTER BOO'S SHELL!
...THAT'S RIGHT.
BUT NOT VERY LIKELY.
THEN YOU WON'T GET ENERGY IF YOU DON'T HURT ME?
...INTER-ESTING.

WELL, LET'S JUST FIND OUT, SHALL WE?
COME AT ME.
HEH HEH
HEE HEE HEE HEE!
...
HYAH !!!!

!!
TK
WK
ZK
UGH !
D
M

READ THIS WAY

!!
OVER HERE, FOOL.
Z-D-D-D-D
HEY. WASN'T POCUS THE CHAMPION OF SOME WORLD ?
THE PLANET ZOON !!
UH...
WHAT THE... ?

READ THIS WAY

THEN PLANET ZOON IT IS!!
PA-PARA-PAA-!
!!
HUH?! WH-WHAT HAPPENED?! WHERE ARE WE ?!
BOBBIDI DID THIS!! HE MAGICALLY TRANS-PORTED THE ROOM...
PROBABLY TO WHERE THE ENEMY HAS THE ADVAN-TAGE!

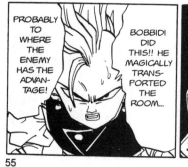

THE GRAVITY HERE IS TEN TIMES THAT OF EARTH!!
HFF... HFF... TH-THIS IS THE END FOR YOU!!
AND I GREW UP HERE!!
FSSH
NOW, REALLY.
DO YOU THINK 10G MEANS ANYTHING TO ME?
Y- YOU'RE BLUFFING !!
!!
WATCH ME.
FSH

READ THIS WAY
!!
HEH
BOOM

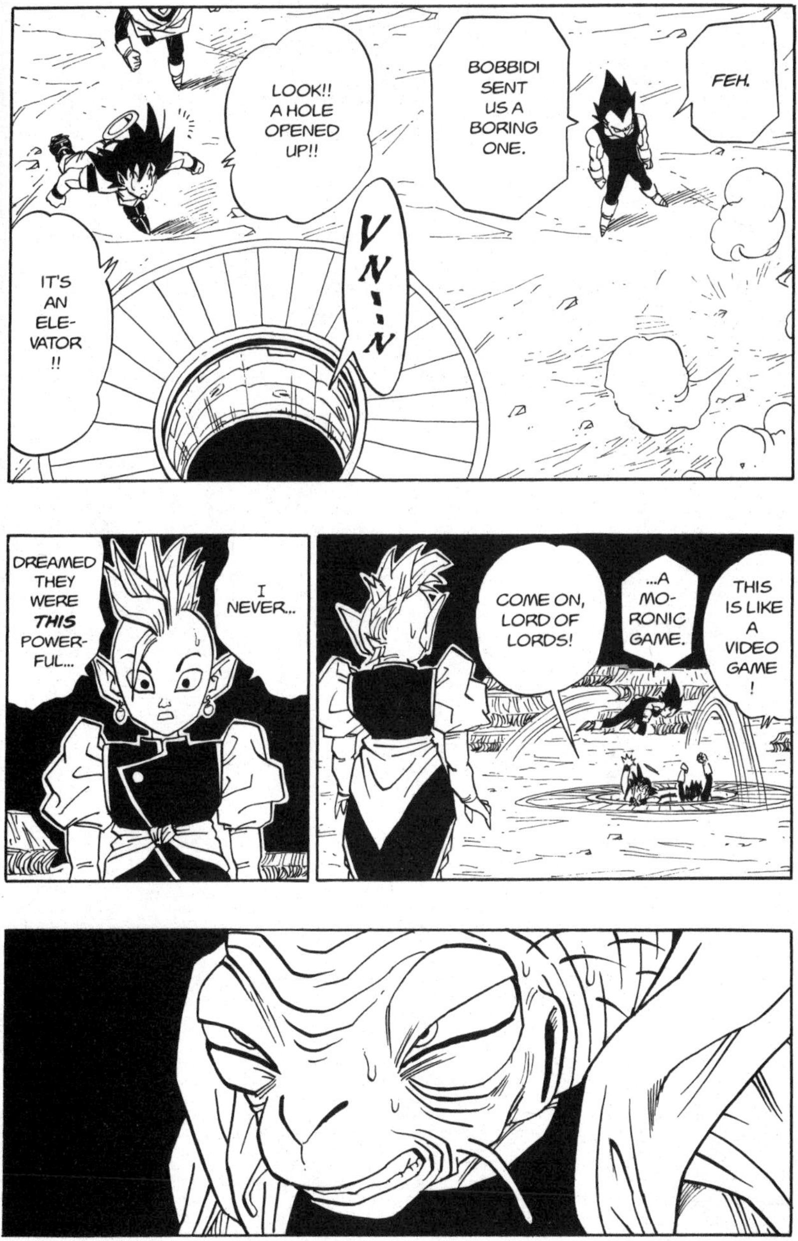

FEH.
BOBBIDI SENT US A BORING ONE.
LOOK!! A HOLE OPENED UP!!
VN--N
IT'S AN ELEVATOR!!
THIS IS LIKE A VIDEO GAME!
...A MORONIC GAME.
COME ON, LORD OF LORDS!
I NEVER...
DREAMED THEY WERE ***THIS*** POWERFUL...

READ THIS WAY

T·T·M
IT LOOKS THE SAME AS BEFORE.
I BET HE'LL CHANGE THE ARENA AGAIN.
HOW COULD EARTHLINGS HAVE SO MUCH POWER?!
THEY WEREN'T LIKE THIS WHEN I CHECKED 300 YEARS AGO...
WELL, THERE ARE THREE STAGES LEFT.
AND IF WORSE COMES TO WORST, I'M STILL HERE!

DBZ:256
Stage Two: Yakon

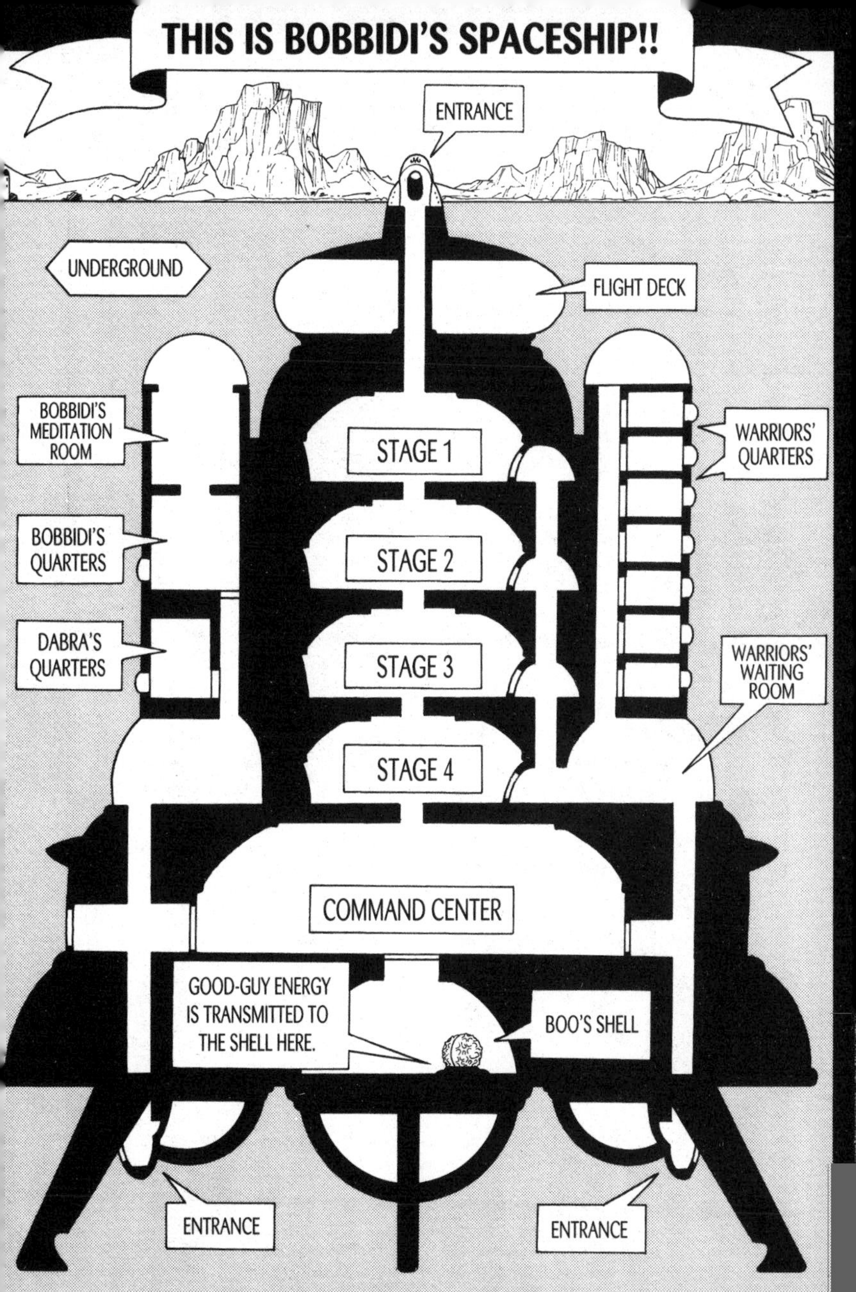
THIS IS BOBBIDI'S SPACESHIP!!
ENTRANCE
UNDERGROUND
FLIGHT DECK
BOBBIDI'S MEDITATION ROOM
STAGE 1
WARRIORS' QUARTERS
BOBBIDI'S QUARTERS
STAGE 2
DABRA'S QUARTERS
STAGE 3
WARRIORS' WAITING ROOM
STAGE 4
COMMAND CENTER
GOOD-GUY ENERGY IS TRANSMITTED TO THE SHELL HERE.
BOO'S SHELL
ENTRANCE
ENTRANCE

READ THIS WAY

WHO SHALL WE HAVE FIGHT IN STAGE TWO?
...
YAKON!
YAKON?!
ALREADY?!
I'M THINKING WE SHOULDN'T UNDER-ESTIMATE THESE EARTH-LINGS.
THEY CLOBBERED POCUS BEFORE HE COULD HURT THEM AT ALL.
...YES. BUT YAKON WILL KILL THEM ALL SO QUICKLY. I WON'T HAVE A CHANCE TO ENJOY MYSELF.

DON'T YOU THINK AWAKENING BOO IS THE PRIORITY RIGHT NOW?
INDEED.
CALL YAKON FOR STAGE TWO!
YES SIR!!
AREN'T THEY READY YET?! HURRY UP!!
THIS IS RIDICULOUS. LET'S JUST DESTROY THE FLOOR AND DROP DOWN!
NO !!
AS I SAID, BOO WILL AWAKEN EVEN IF HE'S NOT YET AT FULL POWER!
PFFF.
I'LL BET THIS BOO ISN'T MUCH TO SPEAK OF, EITHER.
JUST LIKE DABRA.
WHAT ?!
LIKE DABRA...?! WHAT DO YOU MEAN?

READ THIS WAY

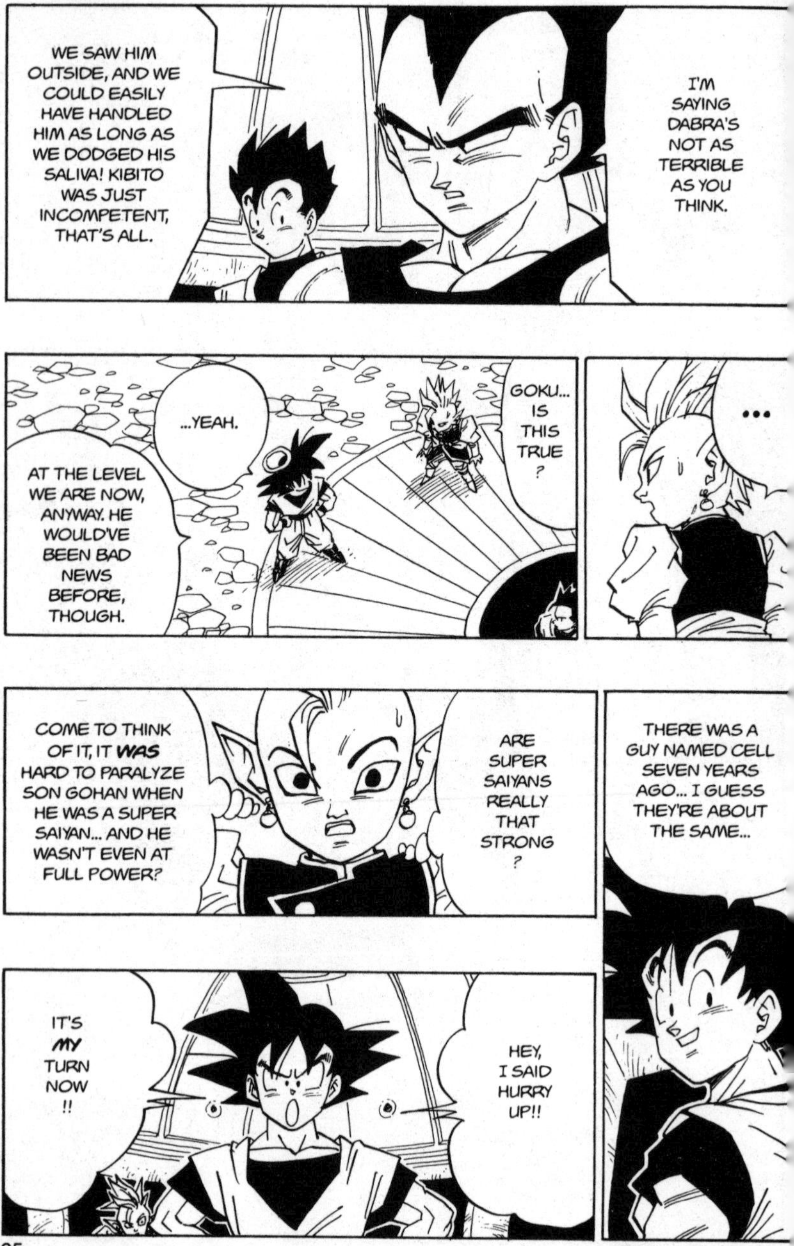

I'M SAYING DABRA'S NOT AS TERRIBLE AS YOU THINK.
WE SAW HIM OUTSIDE, AND WE COULD EASILY HAVE HANDLED HIM AS LONG AS WE DODGED HIS SALIVA! KIBITO WAS JUST INCOMPETENT, THAT'S ALL.
...
GOKU... IS THIS TRUE?
...YEAH.
AT THE LEVEL WE ARE NOW, ANYWAY. HE WOULD'VE BEEN BAD NEWS BEFORE, THOUGH.
ARE SUPER SAIYANS REALLY THAT STRONG?
COME TO THINK OF IT, IT **WAS** HARD TO PARALYZE SON GOHAN WHEN HE WAS A SUPER SAIYAN... AND HE WASN'T EVEN AT FULL POWER?
THERE WAS A GUY NAMED CELL SEVEN YEARS AGO... I GUESS THEY'RE ABOUT THE SAME...
HEY, I SAID HURRY UP!!
IT'S **MY** TURN NOW!!

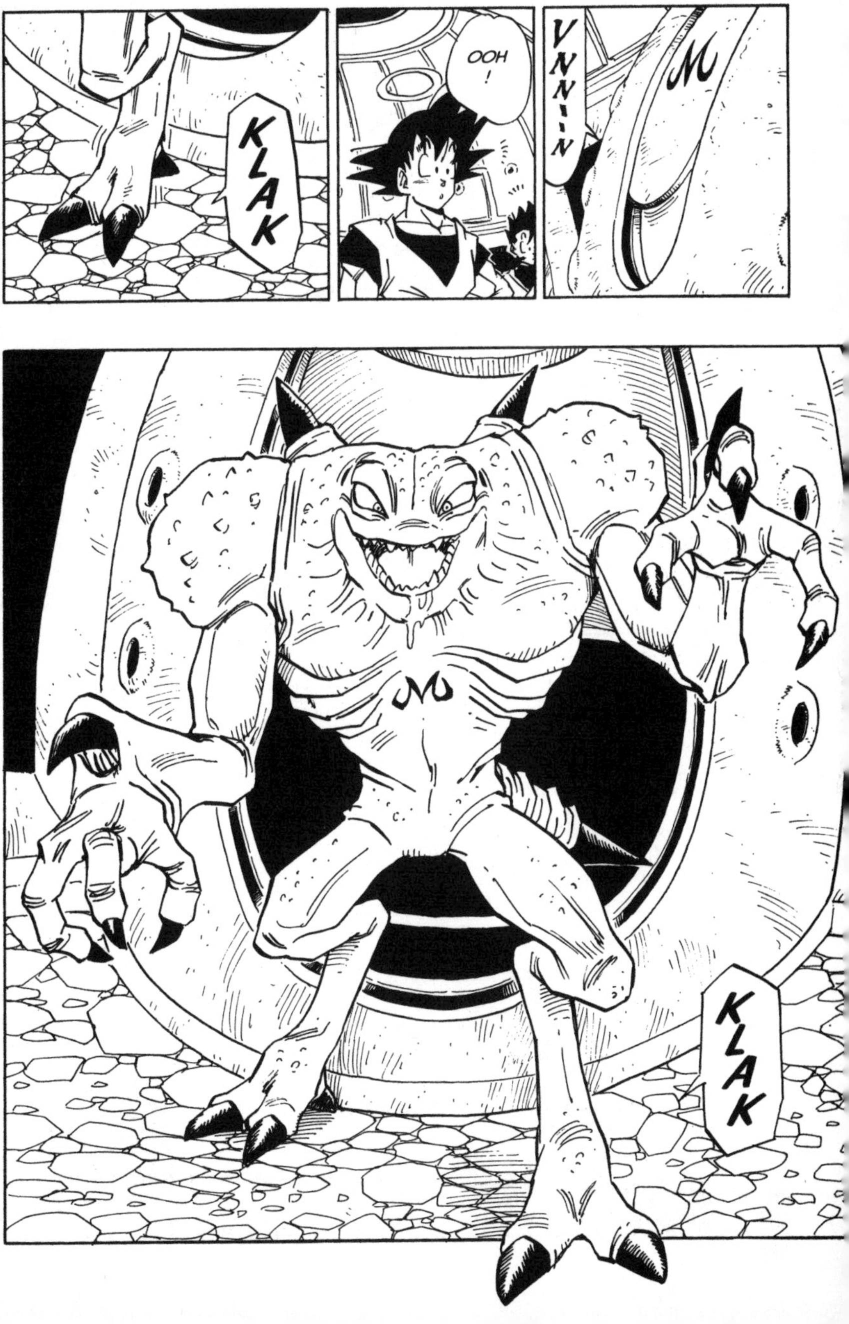
VNNNN
OOH!
KLAK
KLAK

READ THIS WAY

HSSSS
KLAK
HSSSS
HSSSS
GEEZ... WHAT IS *THIS*?!
HO HO HO. WHO SHALL I EAT FIRST?
TRY *ME*!
...HE SURE LOOKS SLOW.
IS THAT YAKON... THE MAGICAL BEAST ?!

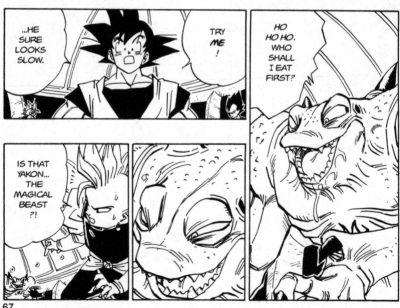

WHOA !!!
HSH
!
PA PA PA PA PA PA PA
PSH
YIKES !!!

READ THIS WAY

TMP
MAN!!
THAT WAS CLOSE!!
HE'S BIG— BUT HE'S FAST!
WE MUST STRIKE TOGETHER!!!
OH, THAT WON'T BE NECESSARY.
DAD'LL BE FINE BY HIMSELF.
...
HEH HEH HEH!!
SO THOSE CLAWS POP OUT, EH?!

HEE HEE! NOW THEY'RE AFRAID!
THIS WILL BE FUN!
GOOD WORK, YAKON!
I KNEW I COULD COUNT ON YOU!
YOU CAN KILL THEM ALL EXCEPT THE LORD OF LORDS! TAKE THEIR ENERGY!
THEN BOO WILL RETURN TO US!!
TO END IT MORE QUICKLY, I'LL TAKE YOU TO YOUR FAVORITE PLACE—THE DARK PLANET!
OOO!
HA HA HA!
BUT DOES YAKON EVEN NEED THE DARK?
MAYBE NOT...
BUT IF THEY DAMAGE THE SHIP, BOO MIGHT AWAKEN AT HALF-STRENGTH.
WE WANT HIM AT FULL POWER!
HEH... SO WE DO!
LET'S GET IT STARTED!
PA-PARA-PAA-!

READ THIS WAY

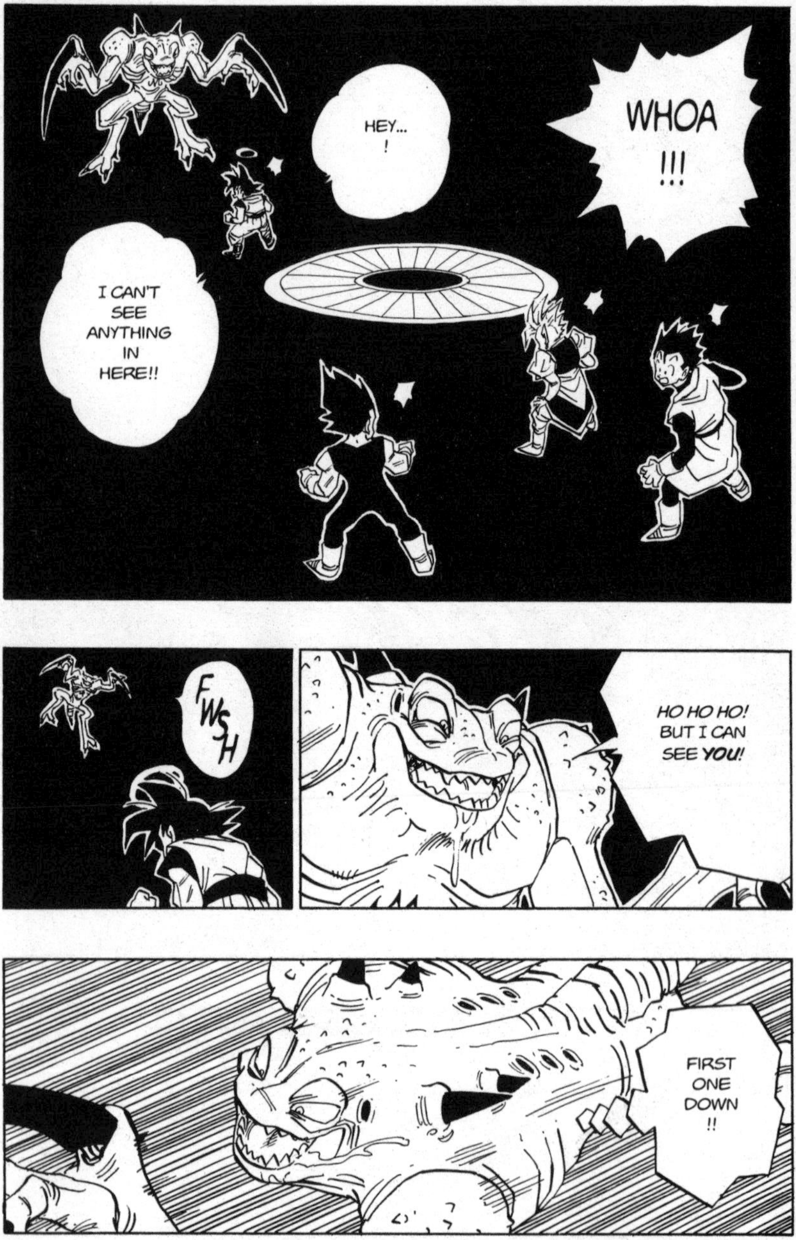

WHOA !!!
HEY... !
I CAN'T SEE ANYTHING IN HERE!!
HO HO HO! BUT I CAN SEE *YOU*!
FWSH
FIRST ONE DOWN !!

SLASH
HUT !!
HUP !!
WAK
...!!!
EH... ?!

READ THIS WAY

WE'RE BETTER'N YOU THINK! EVEN IN THE DARK I CAN TELL WHAT YOU'RE DOING...
BY FEELING THE FLOW OF TINY AIR CUR-RENTS!
...!!
PLUS, THERE ARE OTHER WAYS TO *SEE* YOU...
FWOOOM
!!
SEE? BRIGHT AS DAY!
WHAT *IS* THAT?!

NEXT: More Light!

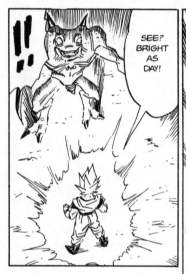

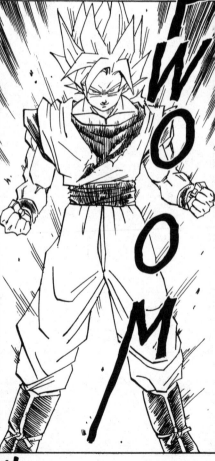

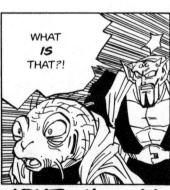

DBZ:257 • Yakon's Treat

READ THIS WAY

YAKON CAN NEVER WIN! HE TOPS OUT AT 800 KIRI!

IT COULD BE A MALFUNCTION... BUT IF HE REALLY DOES HAVE THAT MUCH POWER...

HUH?

AAAAAAn

SWOOO

READ THIS WAY

HEY!!
WHAT?! IT'S DARK AGAIN!!
NO!
HE TRANSFORMED BACK!!
OF COURSE!! YAKON CONSUMES LIGHT ENERGY!!
GOKU'S SUPER SAIYAN ENERGY IS THE PERFECT FOOD!!
BURP
THAT WAS DELICIOUS!!
I'VE NEVER EATEN SUCH FILLING LIGHT!!
YOU EAT IT...?!
DAD, DON'T GO SUPER SAIYAN!! HE EATS LIGHT ENERGY!!
WHAT?!

HEH HEH. YOU HEARD RIGHT. I'D LOVE ANOTHER HELPING IF YOU'LL OBLIGE.
MMM !
I NEVER KNEW LIGHT COULD BE SO TASTY!
...
HMM.
OKAY.
I'LL GIVE IT TO YOU!
WHAT ?!
HERE I GO!
I'M GONNA HANDLE THIS MYSELF !
STAY BACK !!
B M F
WHAT'S HE THINKING... ?
NO, DAD, I'LL FIGHT, TOO! THEN YOU WON'T HAVE TO BE A SUPER SAIYAN !!

HEH HEH!! HOORAY FOR MORONS!!
I'M GONNA EAT MY FILL!!!
HE MUST HAVE A PLAN.
NO. HE IS **NOT** STUPID.
THIS ISN'T A GAME!!!
HE ***IS*** BEING STUPID!! WHY DO YOU ALL INSIST ON FIGHTING ALONE ?!
THERE'S THE SUCTION!!!
NNNN-NGH!!!
KEEP IT COMIN'!!!
SWOOO...

READ THIS WAY

YAKON, YOU FOOL!! WHAT'S THE POINT IF YOU SUCK AWAY HIS ENERGY?!
WE'VE GOT TO SAVE HIS ENERGY FOR BOO!!!! HE'S GOT TO BE HURT!!!
SWOOO...
HEH!
BOOOF

VWOOO

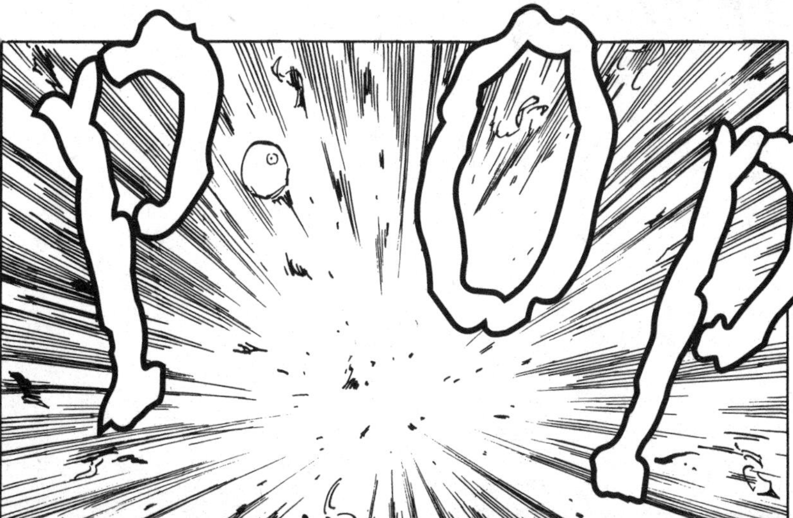
POP

READ THIS WAY

PHEW.
Plep
...
I SEE...
VN--N
HEY, IT OPENED! WE CAN GO DOWN!
...
SO KAKARROT HAS SURPASSED THE SUPER SAIYAN WALL, TOO.
DAD, I FELT THAT CHI!!
THAT WAS AWE-SOME!!
NOT BAD, HUH?

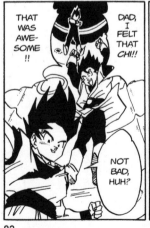

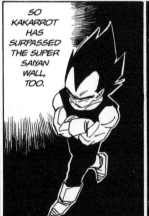

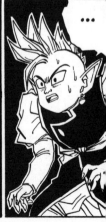

Y-YAKON... BLEW UP...?
BUT WHY...? HOW...?
...
THE BONEHEAD FELL FOR A TRAP.
HE SUCKED IN TOO MUCH ENERGY!
NO... IT LOOKED STRANGE...
THE WAY YAKON SWELLED UP AT THE LAST INSTANT...
THESE AREN'T TYPICAL EARTH-LINGS.

READ THIS WAY

...ALL RIGHT.
I SHALL LAY YOUR WORRIES TO REST.
I'LL GO TO STAGE THREE MYSELF.
BOO'S SHELL WILL OVERFLOW WITH THEIR ENERGY BEFORE YOU KNOW IT.
DABRA... IF YOU GET BEATEN I'M OUT OF WEAPONS.
YOU'D BETTER HAVE A REAL CHANCE.
A CHANCE? *HEH HEH...* I'M THE KING OF THE DEMON PLANE!
NO ONE IS MORE POWERFUL THAN ME!

NEXT: Dabra Takes the Stage!

WE'RE STRONGER THAN HE IS NOW.
HE TOOK PEACE AS AN EXCUSE TO SLACK OFF.
OF COURSE, WE NEVER KNOW WHAT MAY HAPPEN WHEN HE GETS MAD.
HEH HEH HEH...
UHH...
YOU'RE UP NEXT, GOHAN. YOU BEEN TRAINING ?

DBZ:258 · Battle Royale

IT'S HARD TO BELIEVE... THAT MERE MORTALS CAN SHOCK ME LIKE THIS...
N-NO WONDER THESE THREE ARE SO RELAXED... THEY HAVE ACCESS TO INCREDIBLE POWER!
VNNN!N

READ THIS WAY

PSSSH
!!
DABRA... !!
TP...
YOU'VE DEFEATED YAKON AND REACHED STAGE THREE. NOT BAD FOR HUMANS. MIRACULOUS, IN FACT.
BUT THIS IS AS FAR AS YOU GO. YOU'LL HAVE TO DEAL WITH ME NOW.

HO. IF THE TOP DOG IS SHOWING UP ALREADY...
BOBBIDI MUST BE GETTING NERVOUS.
HMPH.
TALK IS FOR PRETENDERS. COME AT ME, ALL OF YOU.
NO WAY !!
IT'S MY TURN !!
...WHAT... ?
DO YOU THINK YOU CAN MAKE A FOOL OF ME?
...
YAK YAK
BLAH BLAH
YADA YADA

READ THIS WAY

UM... AS YOU MAY HAVE NOTICED, SEVERAL OF OUR COMPETITORS HAVE LEFT...
THIS IS AN UNPRECEDENTED SITUATION, AND FRANKLY, WE HAVE NO IDEA HOW TO PROCEED...
MUTTER MUTTER
MURMUR MURMUR
IT'S BEEN ALMOST AN HOUR. THEY SHOULD BE DISQUALIFIED.
BUT ONLY FIVE PEOPLE ARE LEFT...
FEELS LIKE SOMETHING'S UP...
A CLUSTER OF HUGE *CHI* FAR AWAY...
HO! I TOLD YOU THEY WERE AFRAID OF ME!
THE ONES WHO STAYED HAVE REAL COURAGE!
TH-TH-THANK YOU, HERCULE...!
SNORT
OH!
I KNOW!

LADIES AND GENTLE-MEN!!!
FEAR NOT!! THE TOURNAMENT IS NOT RUINED!! AFTER ALL—
DIDN'T YOU COME TO SEE *ME*?!
HEH HEH HEH!
RAAAAAAAAAA
RAH
YAY
YAY
YEAH!!! HERCULE !!!
SHOW US SOME MOVES!!!
WHOOP
YAY
YAY
SAY, I HAVE A GOOD IDEA.
YES, HERCULE?
WHAT IS IT?

READ THIS WAY

A BATTLE ROYALE! DISQUALIFY THE SISSIES, AND THE FIVE BRAVE SOULS WHO REMAIN WILL FIGHT AT THE SAME TIME!
A TOURNAMENT WITH FIVE CONTESTANTS IS A BORE—BUT A FIVE-WAY MELEE WILL GET THE CROWD ROARING!
BUT...
THAT WOULD ONLY...
WHAT, YOU DON'T LIKE MY IDEAS ?!
I CAN LEAVE, TOO, YOU KNOW!
OH, NO! NO !
IT'S A GRAND IDEA!!
GOOD! MAKE THE ANNOUNCEMENT.
EVERYONE, THANKS FOR YOUR PATIENCE!! HERCULE HAS PROPOSED A BATTLE ROYALE AMONG THE FIVE REMAINING CONTESTANTS !!
THEY'LL ALL FIGHT AT THE SAME TIME, AND THE ONE LEFT STANDING WILL BE DECLARED THE CHAMPION !!!
YEAH, THAT'S HERCULE FOR YOU!!!
RAH
WELL SPOKEN !!!
RAH
RAH
HERCULE
WHAT A PROPOSAL. I ADMIRE YOUR COURAGE.
...HUH? COURAGE... ?

A TRUE CHAMPION DOESN'T FEAR SUCH THINGS!!
UH... HA HA HA!
THE OTHER FOUR ARE SURE TO GANG UP ON YOU, SINCE YOU'RE THE TOP CONTENDER!
WELL, OF COURSE.
WHAT WAS I THINKING?!
OH NO...
OF COURSE YOU KNOW THE DEFENDING CHAMPION, HERCULE !!!!
NOW LET'S MEET THE COMPETITORS IN THIS QUINTUPLE MELEE !!!
YAYYAY
RAAAAYAY
I LOVE JEWEL
JEWEL

READ THIS WAY

HERCULE!!!
HERCULE!!!
OH!
TMP
YEAH!!!
RAH RAH
OUR ONLY FEMALE COMPETITOR, NO. 18! (YES, THAT'S HER NAME!)
MIGHTY MASK—LAST TIME HIS RUN ENDED IN THE FIRST ROUND!!
KILLA—HIS *LAST* RUN ENDED IN THE SECOND ROUND!!
AND FINALLY, A FAVORITE WITH THE LADIES—JEWEL, ONE-TIME A RUNNER-UP TO HERCULE!!
RAH RAH
EEEEK!
JEWEL!
HEY.
LET'S ALL KNOCK HERCULE OUT OF BOUNDS FIRST!

D-DOES HE HAVE TWO VOICES...?
...
NO. 18 IS THE ONLY ONE WE'VE GOT TO WATCH.
GO AWAY. WE DON'T CARE ABOUT *HIM*.
YEAH!
BONJOUR, MY DEAR.
WHAT'S A GIRL LIKE YOU DOING IN A MELEE LIKE THIS?
HOW ABOUT DINNER AFTER THE MATCH?
GET BENT.
YOU BUG ME.
WH-WHAT...?!
!!
THIS IS A NO TIME LIMIT BATTLE! NOW, LET'S GET IT STARTED!!
WHOO-HOO!
WHOOP!
YEAH!
HERCULE!
HERCULE!
JEWEL!
YAY
HERCULE

READ THIS WAY

WHD
WHD
EEEEK!! JEWEL !!!
OOH!
EH ?!
EH ?!
ONLY THE TWO PUNY WEAKLINGS ARE LEFT!!! I WIN!!!
WHAT LUCK!!! I DUNNO WHAT HAPPENED, BUT THE TWO I WAS SCARED OF ARE GONE!!!
JEWEL AND KILLA ARE ALREADY ELIMINATED !!!
AMAZING !!

READ THIS WAY
THAT WEIRDO WITH THE LONG TORSO...
...PACKS A POWERFUL PUNCH IN THOSE LITTLE ARMS.
CAREFUL, GOTEN! I HEARD NO. 18 WAS STRONGER THAN OUR DADS ONCE!
I KNOW...!
PSH PSH PSH
PSH PSH
HA HA HA!!!
COME AT ME!!! I'LL TAKE YOU BOTH ON!!!
RRAAHH
RRAAHH
HA HA HA... ...
...
JUST IGNORE HIM...

NEXT: The Championship

DBZ:259 • Mighty Mask Shows His Power!

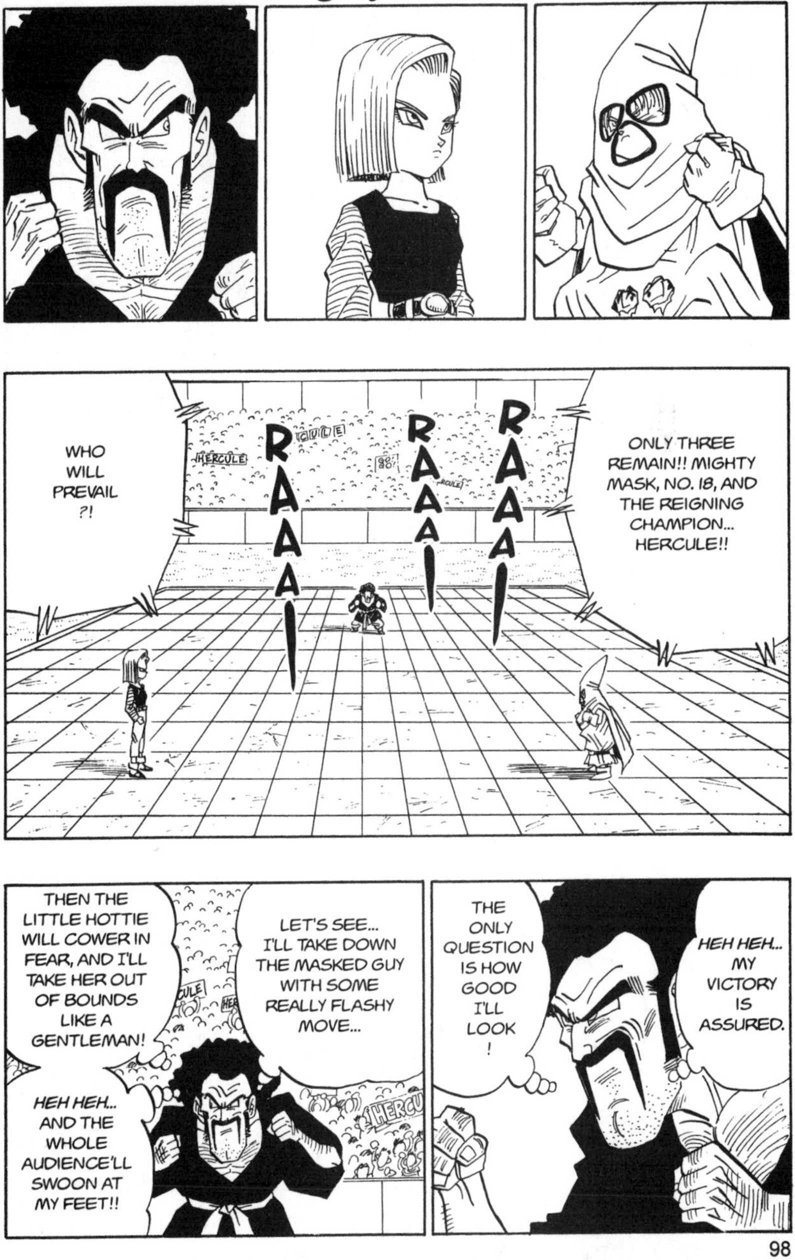
HERCULE
CULE
RAAAA
RAAAA
RAAAA
ONLY THREE REMAIN!! MIGHTY MASK, NO. 18, AND THE REIGNING CHAMPION... HERCULE!!
WHO WILL PREVAIL ?!
HEH HEH... MY VICTORY IS ASSURED.
THE ONLY QUESTION IS HOW GOOD I'LL LOOK !
LET'S SEE... I'LL TAKE DOWN THE MASKED GUY WITH SOME REALLY FLASHY MOVE...
THEN THE LITTLE HOTTIE WILL COWER IN FEAR, AND I'LL TAKE HER OUT OF BOUNDS LIKE A GENTLEMAN!
HEH HEH... AND THE WHOLE AUDIENCE'LL SWOON AT MY FEET!!

READ THIS WAY

TA DA
OHHH
HERCULE HAS PREDICTED VICTORY!!!
YES !!!
I'M SO FINE !!!
WHAT AN IDIOT...
JUST IGNORE HIM.
ALL RIGHT! FIRST, I'M GOING TO TAKE *YOU* DOWN!!
SORRY, BUT THERE'S NO ROOM FOR SOFTIES IN THIS WORLD!!

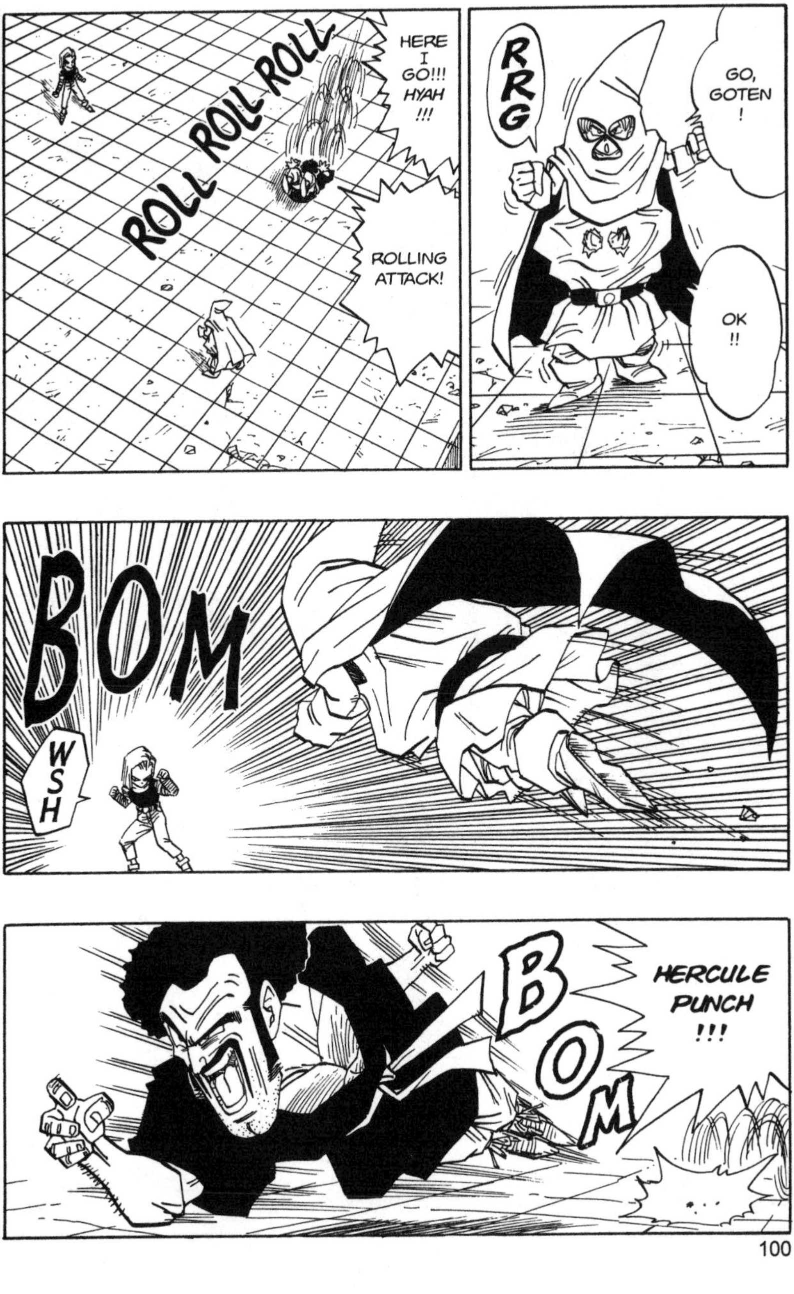
ROLL ROLL ROLL
HERE I GO!!! HYAH!!!
ROLLING ATTACK!
RRG
GO, GOTEN!
OK!!
BOM
WSH
BOM
HERCULE PUNCH!!!

READ THIS WAY

WOK
HERCULE
BASH
NOT THAT WAY! GO RIGHT!
I CAN'T SEE!
BOM
BOM

READ THIS WAY

WOK
WHOA!!! THEY CAN FLY!!! THEY'RE BOTH UP IN THE AIR!!!
WHAT AN AMAZING BATTLE THIS IS!!!
WHEN DID MIGHTY MASK LEARN *THIS*?!
BIP BIP BIP
ARRRGH !!!
IT'S SO HARD TO MOVE-!!!
WOK
EH ?!

H-HE'S DEAD... !!!!
YAAAA !!!
DOOOM!
HERCULE!
BOM
Y'KNOW, GOTEN, YOU COULD KICK HER!
OHH !!!
BUT I CAN'T SEE!
...

READ THIS WAY
WHOA !!!
J-JUMP, GOTEN !!!
POOOM
DOOM
WELL...
I GUESS NO ONE WOULD NOTICE, WITH THIS COS-TUME...
SHOOT!!! WE'LL NEVER WIN THIS WAY!!!
HEY TRUNKS! LET'S GO SUPER SAIYAN!

YOU'RE ON!
YAY!
WHAT A WEIRDO... HIS LIMBS ARE TOO SMALL FOR HIS BODY... BUT HE'S SO STRONG...
...
BOOM
!!
VOOOOOOO
WE'RE STILL AT A DIS-ADVANTAGE— WE SHOULD GO WITH CHI BLASTS!
CHI?! ARE YOU SURE...?
YEAH! IT WON'T KILL HER!
THAT'S NO. 18!

READ THIS WAY
...OH-HO...! SUPER SAIYAN!
NOW I KNOW WHO YOU ARE... BOYS.
DON'T USE FULL POWER!
I KNOW!
VSH
BAM

!!
UNH !!!!
HYOW
FLASH

Y-YOU'VE GOTTA BE KIDDING ME... THAT SPEED...THAT POWER...

ARE THOSE TWITS REALLY *THAT* GOOD...?

FOO-EY! I MIS-SED!

LET'S BOMBARD HER!

... ...

I'M GONNA WIN THIS !!
TRUNKS! GOTEN !
GACK !!!!
I BETTER END THIS QUICK !
IN THAT CASE–
HSSH
SHE...
SHE KNOWS !!!
RRIP
YEEE !!!
YAAA !!!!

READ THIS WAY

YOOON
NO!!! MIGHTY MASK...
HAS BEEN RIPPED IN TWO !!!
...WAIT... NO... !!
DUMMY!! WHY'D YOU GO *THAT* WAY?!
TH- THERE ARE TWO OF THEM... !!!
SO *THAT'S* WHERE THEY WENT !
HEE-HEE! JUST LIKE I FIGURED !
R-RUN !!!
NO TEAMS ALLOWED!!! YOU'RE DISQUALIFIED !!!!
PHEW~
NOW IT'S JUST NO. 18 AND HERCULE !!
THE WINNER WILL BE THE NEW CHAMPION !!!!
TM
I'M
...SO DEAD...

DBZ:260 • We Have a Winner!!!

HA HA HA!! IT'S ALL OURS!!
LUCKY YOU! YOUR MOM'S GONNA BE RICH!
THIS IS NO LAUGHING MATTER!
WE DON'T KNOW WHAT'S HAPPENING TO THE OTHERS...
HUH?
HOW'D SHE FIGURE IT OUT...?
DRAT...
VIDEL!
IT'S VIDEL!!
GOTEN!!
OH!

READ THIS WAY

READ THIS WAY

GOMP
GYAAAH !!!!!!
FLAP FLAIL
PL-PL-PLEASE!!!
D-DON'T KILL ME!!!
I'LL DO ANYTHING!!!!
QUIT SCREAMING, IDIOT—
OR I REALLY WILL KILL YOU!
NO. 18 HAS A HEADLOCK ON HERCULE!!
NOW LISTEN TO ME.
DO YOU WANT TO WIN?
N-NO... THAT'S OK...!
JUST DON'T HURT ME...!!
I COULD *LET* YOU WIN...
HUH?!
GIVE ME 20 MILLION ZENI AND IT'S YOURS.
IT'S NOT A BAD PRICE...TO KEEP YOUR REPUTATION.

READ THIS WAY

HEH HEH HEH.. !
...HEH...
AGGH !!
...
HOH !!
FSH FSH
HYAH HYAH HYAH !!
THIS IS STILL THE AGE OF HERCULE !!!
YOU'RE PRETTY GOOD...BUT YOU CAME UP AGAINST THE WRONG MAN!!
THIS IS YOUR FINISH !!!
OHH.. !!!
IS THIS FOR REAL ?
HERCULE
HA HA HA! I'VE SEEN THROUGH YOUR TECHNIQUES!! TOO BAD— FOR YOU!!

READ THIS WAY

JUST DO IT, CLOWN.
UH...
Y-YES MA'AM !
HYAAH !!!
HERCULE MIRACLE SPECIAL ULTRA SUPER MEGATON PUNCH !!!!
BWOK

R-RIGHT IN THE FACE!!

WHOA!!!

...M-MORE OR LESS...

W-WELL...

...*THIS* IS YOUR KILLER MOVE?

DMM

WAAH!!

HSSH

...UH...

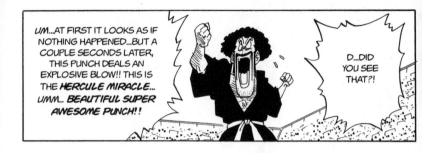

D...DID YOU SEE THAT?!
UM...AT FIRST IT LOOKS AS IF NOTHING HAPPENED...BUT A COUPLE SECONDS LATER, THIS PUNCH DEALS AN EXPLOSIVE BLOW!! THIS IS THE HERCULE MIRACLE... UMM.. BEAUTIFUL SUPER AWESOME PUNCH!!
HERCULE WINS !!!
PAAAA
I'M NUMBER ONE !!!!!

NO. 18 SHOWED ASTONISHING PROWESS, BUT SHE WAS NO MATCH FOR HERCULE!!! HE DEFENDS HIS TITLE!!!
RAAA!
RAAA!
YOU'RE AWE-SOME, HERCULE!!
SAVIOR OF THE WORLD!!
I'LL BE AT YOUR HOUSE TOMORROW TO PICK UP THE MONEY.
IF I DON'T GET IT, YOU'RE DEAD.
RAAA!
RAAA!
RAAA!
HER-CULE!
...Y-YES MA'AM.
D-DON'T WORRY...
HER-CULE!
HER-CULE!
...SO THERE YOU GO.
THAT'S WHERE THEY WENT.
FIGHT

READ THIS WAY

OO!
...
OO! OO!
WARLOCKS... GENIES...
OO!
WOW...
DID YOU HEAR THAT, GOTEN?
YEAH!
HA HA.. HA HA HA HA..
WOW! THAT'S SO COOL!
IT IS, ISN'T IT?!
WHAT?!
FIGHT

THAT WAY, RIGHT ?!
YEAH, I FEEL THEIR CHI!!
W-WAIT! WHERE DO YOU DO THINK YOU'RE GOING... ?!
HURRY !!!
BEFORE THEY BEAT ALL THE BAD GUYS!
NO WAY, I WANNA SEE !!!
I WANNA SEE BOO THE GENIE !!!
GO !!!!!
VMMM
VMMMM
RRRG

V-V-VOOSH
YEE HAW !!!! WOO-HOO !!!!
DOOM
DOOM
...NO WAY...
...
FIGHT

WHO'S THE STRONGEST UNDER THE HEAVENS?!

DBZ:261 • A Wicked Soul Revealed

EVEN AS HERCULE CELEBRATED HIS VICTORY, GOHAN AND DABRA WERE LOCKED IN COMBAT...
B-B-BAM

WOK
HST~~
ZSSH
VOOM

READ THIS WAY
HOOO
NNH !!!
HWAH
VVN
WHF
HUH ?!

I'M
OVER
HERE
!!!!
!!
BOOM
DOOM

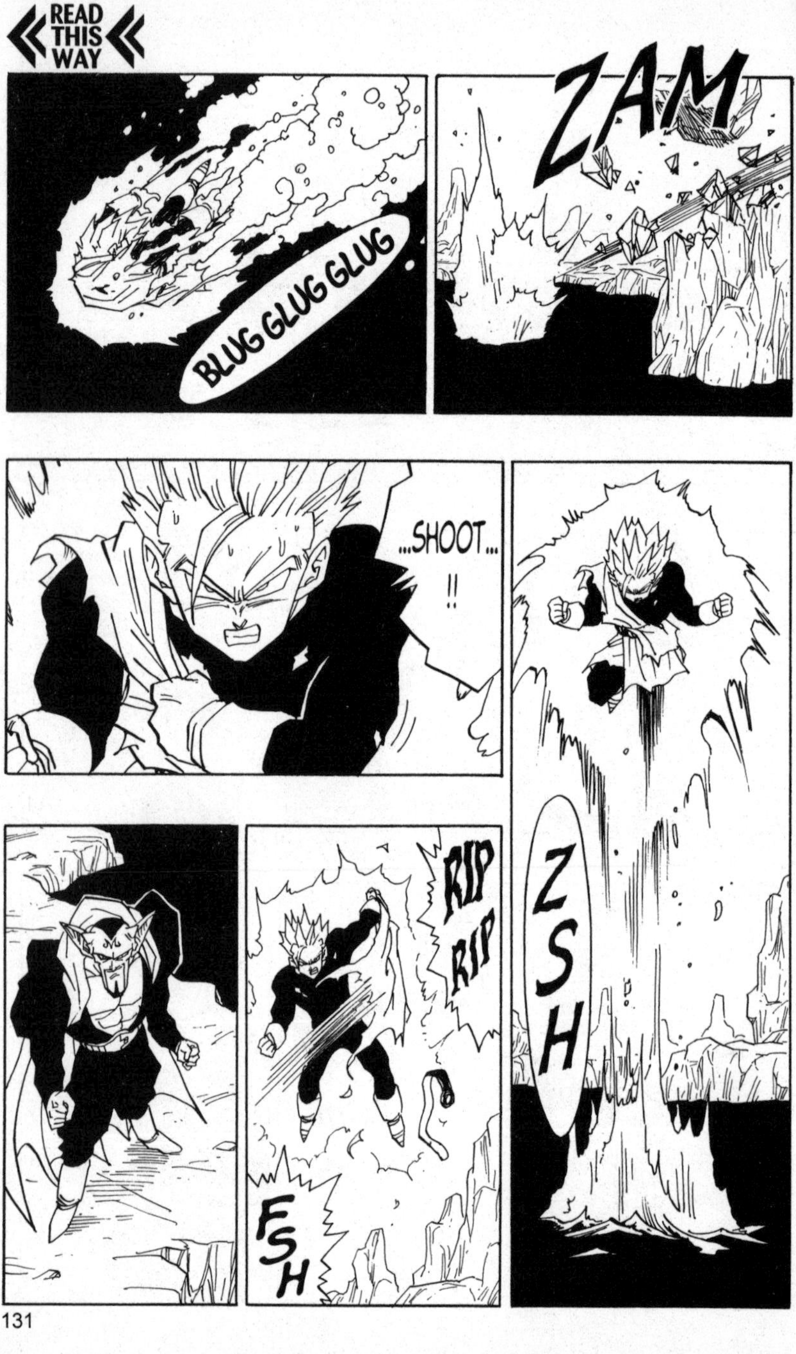
READ THIS WAY
ZAM
BLUG GLUG GLUG
...SHOOT...!!
ZSH
RIP RIP
FSH

SO HE USES MAGIC, HUH?
HE'S TOUGHER THAN I THOUGHT.
HMPH...
I'M LOSING PATIENCE...
HE REALLY HAS BEEN SLACKING!
GOHAN WAS STRONGER WHEN HE WAS A KID...
HE STILL SHOULDN'T HAVE THIS MUCH TROUBLE WITH HIM... PATHETIC...
DYAAH!!!!!!!!!

READ THIS WAY
PTUI
BWUCH
WATCH OUT!! YOU'LL BE TURNED TO STONE!!!
WHOA !!!
FSH
BRAK

VNN
!!
!!

READ THIS WAY

BLAST IT...!
COME ON, DABRA...!
YOU HAVE TO DAMAGE HIM MORE!
...IF ONLY BOO WOULD AWAKEN... HE'D FINISH THEM ALL!
NOW I'M ANNOYED!
I'LL FINISH IT FOR HIM!!
C'MON, VEGETA, LET HIM DO IT! HE'S STILL GOT A CHANCE!
I DON'T CARE ABOUT ANY OF THIS!!

READ THIS WAY

I JUST WANT TO GET IT OVER WITH AND FIGHT YOU!!
THAT'S WHY I WENT TO THAT STUPID TOURNAMENT!!
HEH!!
...?!
MASTER BOBBIDI!! TAKE US BACK TO THE SHIP!
I'VE MADE A GREAT DISCOVERY!!
EH ?!
ONE THAT WILL SURELY AWAKEN BOO!!

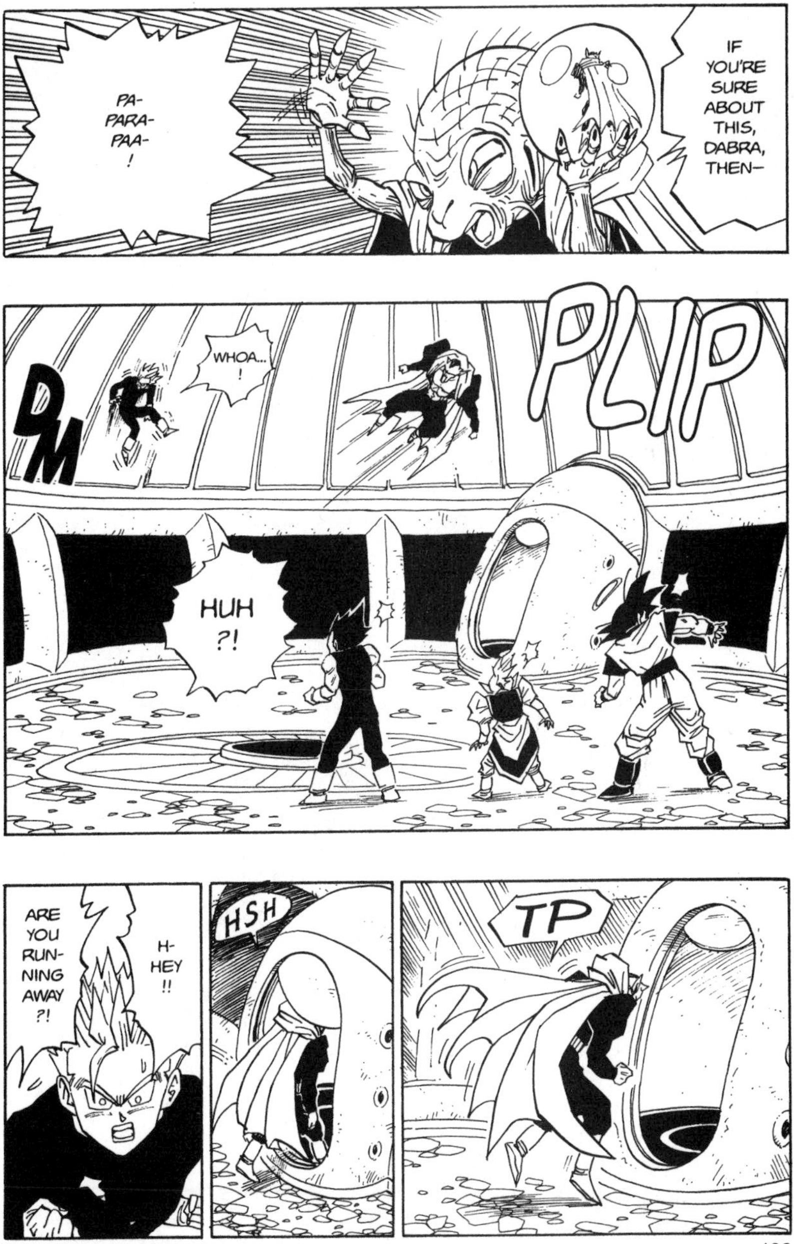
IF YOU'RE SURE ABOUT THIS, DABRA, THEN—
PA-PARA-PAA-!
PLIP
WHOA...!
DM
HUH?!
ARE YOU RUNNING AWAY?!
H-HEY!!
HSH
TP

THE... WHAT... ?!
FSSH
RUNNING AWAY? HEH.. NO...
I JUST DON'T NEED TO MESS WITH YOU—BECAUSE I'VE FOUND THE PERFECT FIGHTER!
WHAT'S THIS ABOUT, DABRA?
IT BETTER BE GOOD.
IT IS!
ONE OF THEM HAS A VERY WICKED SOUL...
...SURELY WICKED ENOUGH TO TURN TO OUR SIDE!
...AHHH! SO WE MAKE THEM FIGHT EACH OTHER—AND TAKE THEIR ENERGY!!!
THAT SHOULD WAKE BOO UP!!!

NEXT: *Mortal Enemies!*

DBZ:262 · Goku vs. Vegeta

...I'M NOT SURE. HE SAID HE FOUND A FIGHTER...
WH-WHAT DID HE SAY...?!
OH !
WHAT DOES THAT MEAN... ?!
"FOUND" ?!

READ THIS WAY

WA HA HA!! YOU'RE RIGHT!! THIS ONE'S NOT LIKE THE OTHERS !!
HIS HEART IS DRIPPING WITH EVIL! HE DIDN'T COME HERE TO DO GOOD!!
HE'S JUST WHAT WE NEED!!
HAAH- !!!

!!
!!
AARRRH...!!!
I KNEW IT !!!
!!
BMMM
GUHH...!!!!
...!!!!

READ THIS WAY

UNH... GRR... !!!
VEGETA !!
BOBBIDI'S TRYING TO USE THE EVIL IN YOU!!!
EMPTY YOUR MIND!!! DON'T THINK ABOUT ANYTHING !!
SH- SHUT... UP... !!!
DON'T... ORDER ME... !!!
HEE HEE HEE!! YOU'RE MINE!! NOW TO BRING OUT YOUR LATENT POWERS— !!
ARRRH...!!
BIRI
BIRI
NO, VEGETA!! DON'T LET HIM CONTROL YOU !!!

VEGETA... !!
NH... NNNH...
HUHH...
OH NO... !!
!!

SUPERB, SUPERB!
I HAVE THE PERFECT PLACE TO MAKE THEM FIGHT!
PA-PARA-PAA-!
PIP
WHAT ?!
天下一武道会

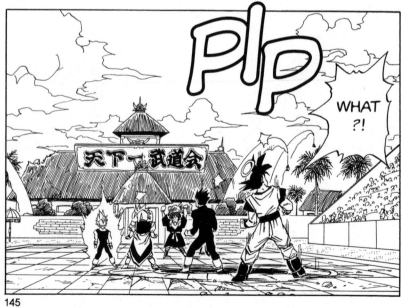

WE'RE BACK AT THE TOURNA-MENT...!!
YOU'RE TOO LATE!! THE CONTEST IS OVER!!
WH-WHO ARE THEY?!
THEY CAME OUTTA NOWHERE...!!
COME ON NOW... WHAT WAS YOUR NAME? YES...VEGETA!! STEAL ENERGY FROM THEM! THEN KILL THEM— IF YOU WANT!

READ THIS WAY

SHUT UP! I'M ONLY AFTER KAKARROT!
THE REST CAN JUST BLOW AWAY!
I...I CAN'T BELIEVE HIM... HE'S STILL NOT UNDER MY FULL CONTROL...?!
I'VE NEVER SEEN A WILL SO STRONG! WELL, NO MATTER...
IT *IS* THEM!!
WHAT'S GOING ON...?!
TH-THESE GUYS...!!! THEY'RE... THEY'RE FROM THAT BATTLE WITH CELL!
NO WAY... THEY'RE STILL ALIVE...?!

H-HEY!
ZZIP
DOOM

READ THIS WAY
YOU IDIOT... !!!!
PCH
GAH !!!!
!!

ZWOO
D-ZOOM
...!!!!

READ THIS WAY
HERCULE
WAAAAH !!!
RUN !!!
YEEE !
HE DIDN'T...
V-
VEGETA... !!

DBZ:263 · Vegeta's Pride

HE'S GONNA KILL US ALL!!
LET'S GET OUTTA HERE!
GAAA!
EEK!
OUTTA MY WAY!
WHAT'S WRONG WITH YOU?!
VEGETA!!
UH... UHH...
WA HA HA!
HE MUST'VE KILLED 200 ALREADY!!

READ THIS WAY

VEGETA !!
WHAT HAVE YOU DONE ?!
NOW, KAKARROT... FIGHT ME.
UNLESS YOU WANT TO ADD MORE CORPSES TO THE PILE, THAT IS!
...VEGETA... DID YOU...
...LET BOBBIDI CONTROL YOU ON PURPOSE... ?

VNNN
...
BM
HOOOM
!!

READ THIS WAY

SON GOKU!!!
D-DON'T DO IT!!!
THIS IS WHAT BOBBIDI WANTS!! HE'LL ABSORB YOUR ENERGY AND WAKE BOO!!!
BOOOM

READ THIS WAY

VEGETA... YOU SURRENDERED TO BOBBIDI'S SPELL ON PURPOSE...TO MAKE ME FIGHT.
AM I RIGHT ?
WHA...
WHAT... ?!
IF I HADN'T, I'D NEVER GET TO FIGHT YOU. AFTER TODAY YOU'RE LEAVING THIS WORLD FOREVER.
JUST... TO FIGHT HIM... ?
ARE YOU THAT INSANE... ?!
"INSANE"... ?! YOU THINK THIS IS "INSANE" ?!
WHO CARES ABOUT BOO?!! THIS IS WHAT I LIVE FOR!!!

...HE... SURPASSED ME...!!
HE'S SAIYAN JUST LIKE ME, BUT HE FAR OUT-STRIPPED ME!!
ME—THE PRINCE!! THE STRONGEST OF THEM ALL!!!
ONCE... HE EVEN SAVED MY LIFE !!!
I CAN'T STAND IT !!!!
...I CAN'T... !!!!
...

READ THIS WAY

BOBBIDI!!! TAKE US SOME-PLACE WHERE THERE'S NO PEOPLE!
THEN I'LL FIGHT HIM!!!
!!
...!!!
WAIT!!!!
YOU'LL HAVE TO DEFEAT ME FIRST!!

!!
SHFF
...

READ THIS WAY

D...
DAD...
...
SORRY, LORD OF LORDS.
ALL RIGHT...
DO AS YOU WISH...
SERVES YOU RIGHT, KAIÔ-SHIN!
HEE HEE! THEY'RE AT EACH OTHER'S THROATS!
SO— I'LL TELEPORT YOU, LIKE YOU ASKED!
PA-PARA-PAA!

BIP
I WAS JUST GOING TO MAKE THEM PAY!!
C... CURSES!
WELL... NEXT TIME!
WHAT...?!
HUH...?
THEY'RE GONE...
SON GOHAN AND I WILL BREAK THROUGH THIS ENTRANCE AND GO TO FIGHT BOBBIDI AND DABRA.
FIGHT IT OUT TO YOUR HEART'S CONTENT.

READ THIS WAY

BOO MAY BE AWAKENED BY THIS SHOCK, BUT WE CAN'T HELP IT.
IT WILL BE BETTER THAN IF HE REACHES FULL POWER WITH THE ENERGY HE'LL ABSORB FROM YOU.
IF WE'RE LUCKY, WE MAY BE ABLE TO STOP THEM FIRST.
...
HO HO HO! NO YOU DON'T!!
VEGETA, STOP THEM! KILL EVERYONE WHO GETS IN THE WAY!!
NNH...!!
UNH... NRAAUGH...
URRH... HFF HFF...!!
WELL?! DO IT!!
I... WILL ***NOT***...!!
THEY HAVE NOTHING TO DO... WITH MY BATTLE...!!

DBZ:264 •Two Battles to the Death

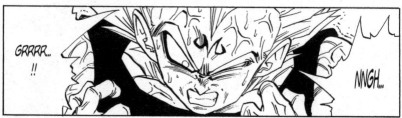

!!
WHAT ?!
...
I'LL ONLY SAY IT ONCE MORE— KILL THE LORD OF LORDS!
NOW, VEGETA !!
NNGH...
GRRRR... !!

I...AM THE PROUD...
...PRINCE OF THE SAIYANS...!
AND I... SAY THIS...! I ONLY WANT TO FIGHT... KAKARROT!
HF
HF
...
I WILL NEVER BE YOUR SERVANT!!!
YOU MAY TAKE OVER MY BODY AND SOUL– BUT NOT MY PRIDE!!!
THIS...HAS NEVER HAPPENED...
...SO MUCH PRIDE...
IT DOESN'T MATTER.
HE'LL STILL HELP US GET ENERGY.

READ THIS WAY

THE LORD OF LORDS CAN'T DO ANYTHING WITH ME AROUND.
BESIDES, YOU WANTED TO SEE HIM DIE BEFORE YOUR VERY EYES... MM?
I CAN'T BELIEVE A MORTAL CAN BE IN BOBBIDI'S CONTROL... YET STILL DEFY HIM...
VEGETA... YOU WANTED TO FIGHT ME...
...THAT MUCH?
PERHAPS WE SHOULD OPEN THE PASSAGE.
OTHERWISE THEY MAY FORCE IT OPEN, AND AWAKEN BOO BY SHAKING THE SHIP.
MMM...
MAYBE SO...
VNNN

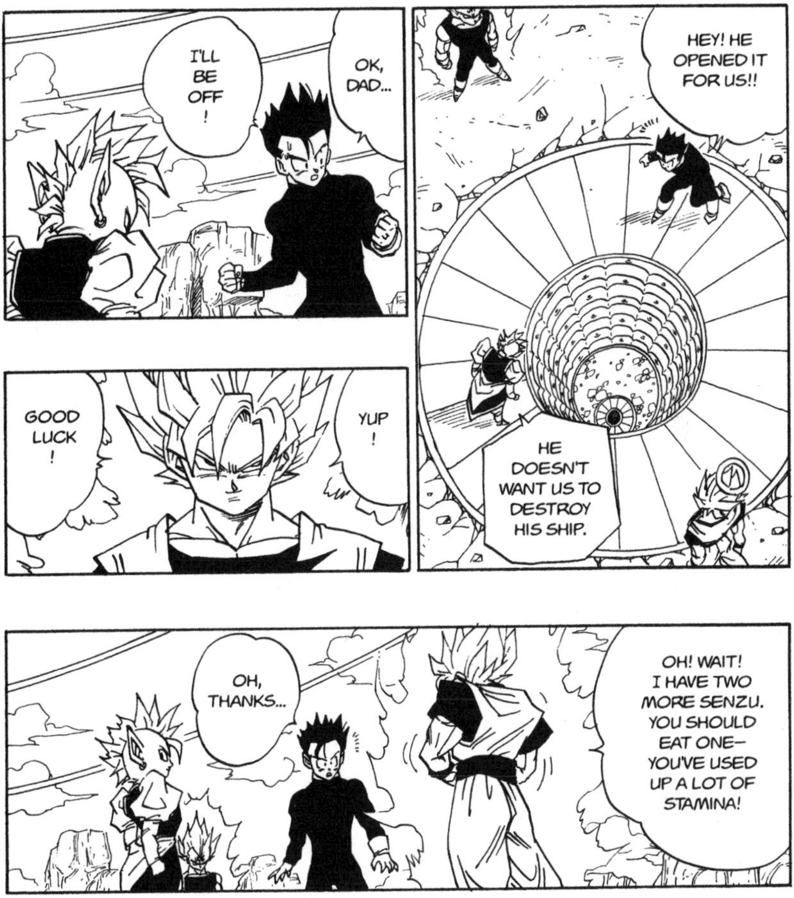

168

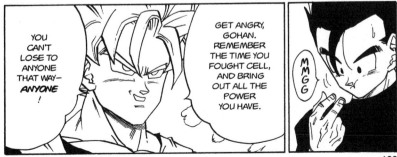

READ THIS WAY

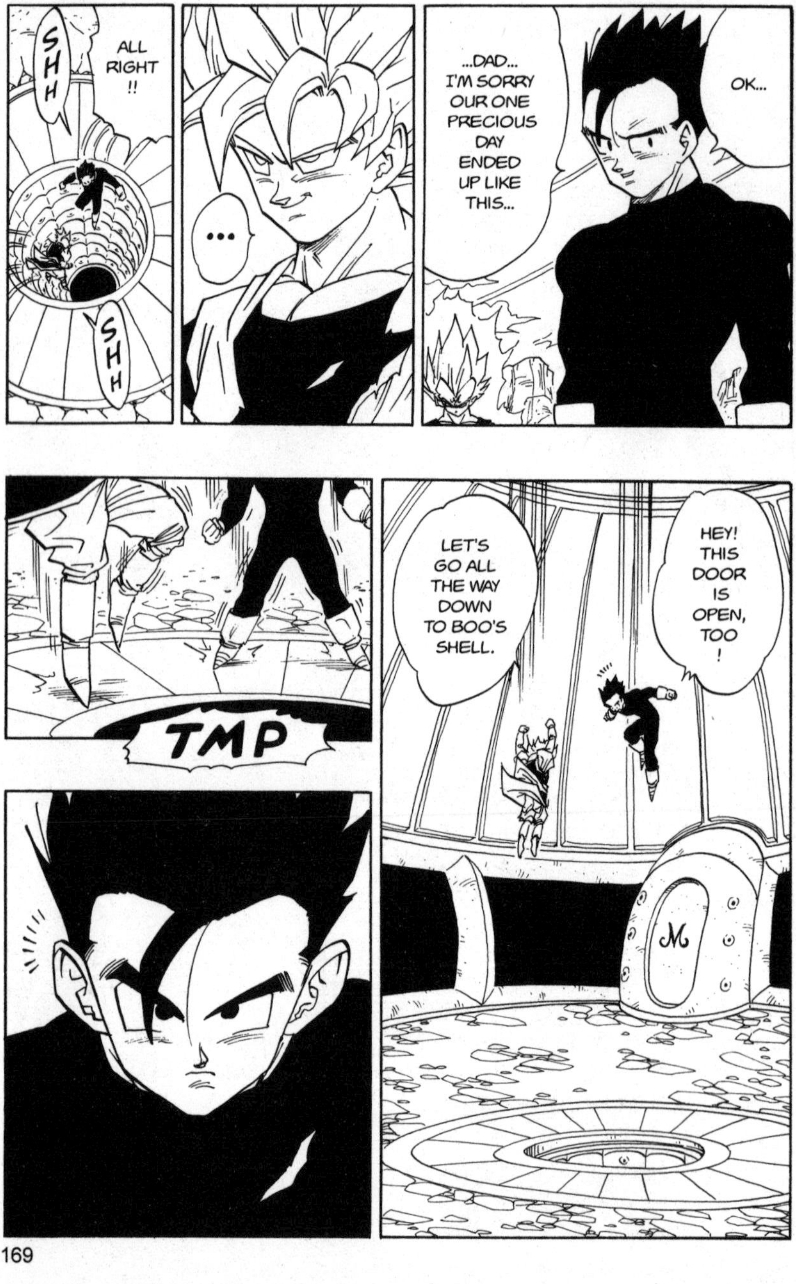
OK...
...DAD... I'M SORRY OUR ONE PRECIOUS DAY ENDED UP LIKE THIS...
...
ALL RIGHT !!
SHH
SHH
HEY! THIS DOOR IS OPEN, TOO !
LET'S GO ALL THE WAY DOWN TO BOO'S SHELL.
TMP

WELCOME.
WEL-COME, LORD OF LORDS...
...YOU, WHO KILLED MY FATHER...
I'VE COME TO DEFEAT YOU, BOBBIDI...
...AND STOP BOO'S AWAKEN-ING.
...THAT'S BOO'S SHELL... ?
YES...

READ THIS WAY

I DON'T THINK THAT'LL BE SO EASY. I HAVE DABRA ON MY SIDE.
HEH HEH HEH~
LET'S HURRY. BOO MAY BE ABSORBING ENERGY AS WE SPEAK.
OK...!
I'LL FIGHT BOBBIDI!
HYOOOO

I'M GOING TO END THIS QUICKLY, AT FULL POWER.
I DON'T WANT TO GET HURT AND GIVE BOO ANY ENERGY.
I'M LOOKING FORWARD TO SEEING THE FRUITS OF YOUR TRAINING IN THE AFTERLIFE...
DMM
PRETTY GOOD.
YOU'RE STRONGER THAN GOHAN!

READ THIS WAY
DOOM
KAH !!!
!
I GUESS THIS WON'T BE SO QUICK...
COME ON !!!
I'LL KILL YOU !!!

HYU
DOM
BZZT BZZT
NNH...
!!!
ZIP

DOM
BWOK
BOK
KABOOK

WHAM
RRG
UNH... !!!
WOK
RAAH !!!!

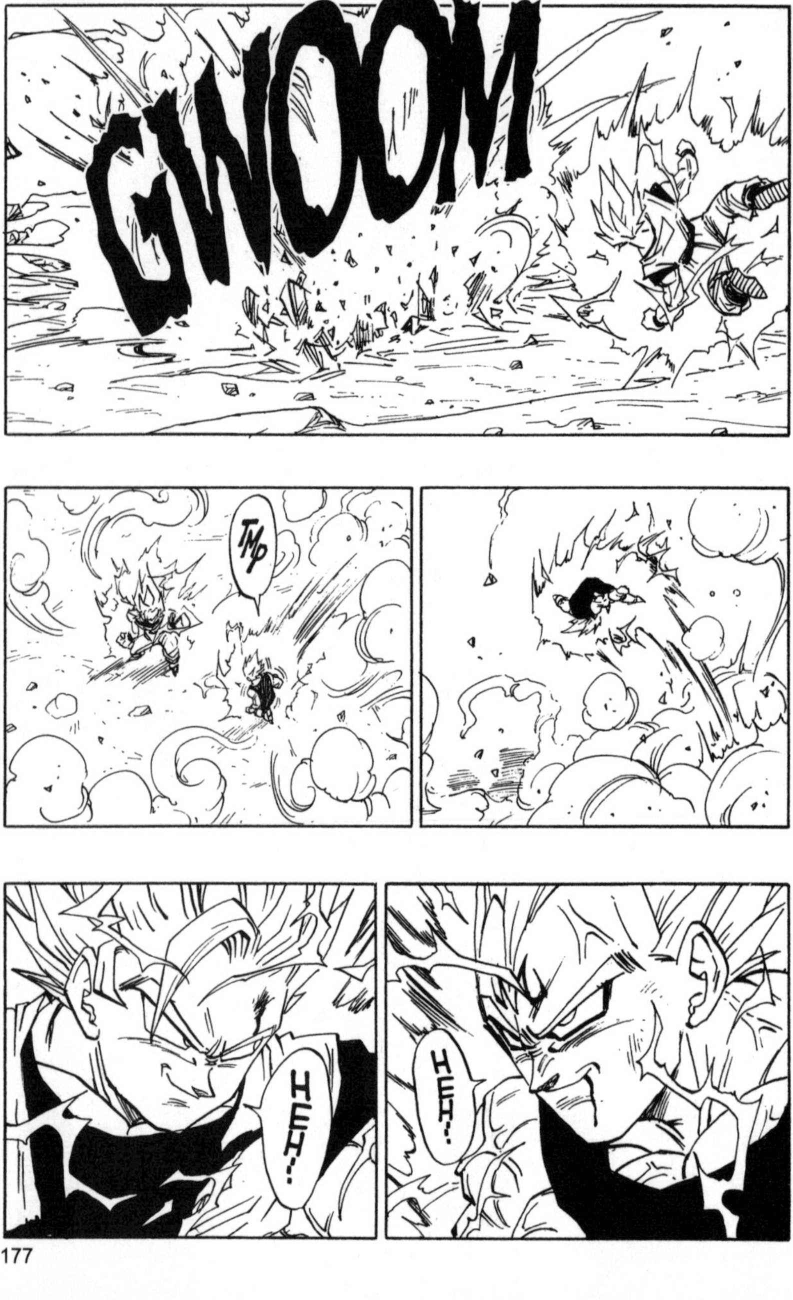
GWOOM
TMP
HEH...
HEH...

DBZ:265 • Countdown

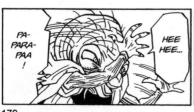

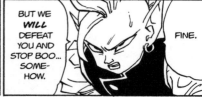

PIP
IT WON'T BE HARD TO DISPOSE OF THIS LITTLE SNOT.
OF COURSE. I FOUGHT HIM EARLIER.
JUST TO MAKE SURE...DABRA, YOU CAN DEFEAT THAT EARTHLING, RIGHT?
GET ANGRY, GOHAN... REMEMBER THE TIME YOU FOUGHT CELL, AND BRING OUT ALL THE POWER YOU HAVE.
YOU CAN'T LOSE TO ANYONE THAT WAY—ANYONE!
...

READ THIS WAY

I AM ANGRY...! BUT STILL...
I CAN'T BE THE WAY I WAS THEN...
BMMM
HEE HEE... HEAR THAT, LORD OF LORDS? YOU CAN'T KILL ME LIKE YOU KILLED MY DADDY!
I HAVE FAR MORE MAGICAL POWER THAN HIM! AND I HAVE DABRA WITH M–
PII PI-PII PIIII I
WHAT ?!

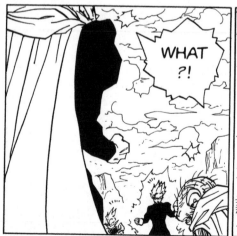

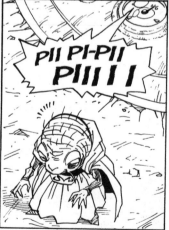

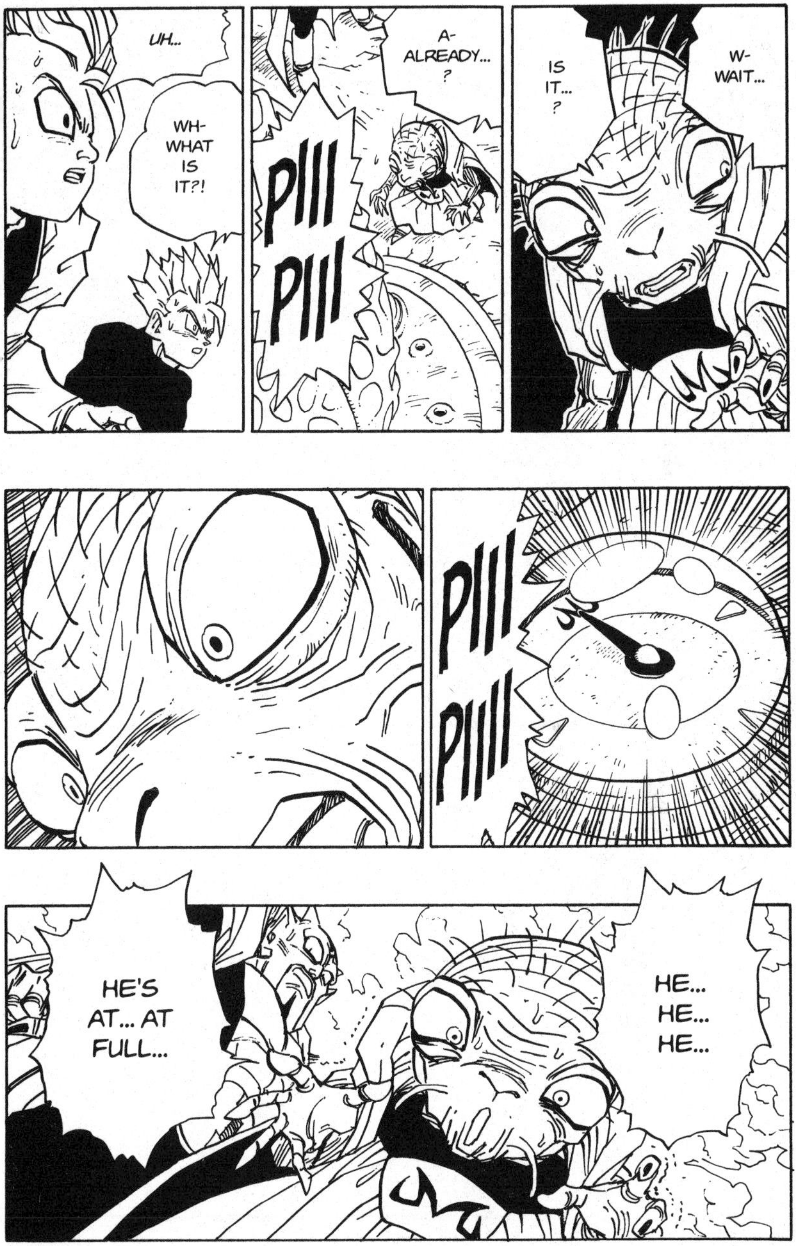
UH...
WH- WHAT IS IT?!
A- ALREADY... ?
PIII PIII
W- WAIT...
IS IT... ?
PIII PIIII
HE'S AT... AT FULL...
HE... HE... HE...

READ THIS WAY

HE'S AT FULL POWER!!!!!
BOO'S AT FULL POWER !!!!
!!
HE'LL FINALLY AWAKEN !!!!

WH- WHAT... ?!
H-HOW COULD THIS BE...? DID THEY DEAL THIS MUCH DAMAGE ALREADY... ?!
...I GET IT NOW...!! DAD'S FIGHTING AT A POWER LEVEL BEYOND THE SUPER SAIYAN LIMITS... AND PROBABLY VEGETA TOO... SO THE DAMAGE IS GREATER...!!!
I-I CAN'T BELIEVE IT...!!! THE WORST CASE SCENARIO... !!
...I MISCAL- CULATED EVERY- THING... !!

READ THIS WAY

KKM
FFFFFF
D-D-DMM
RRRMMMM

READ THIS WAY
H-HEY... THIS IS SOME INCREDIBLE CHI...
WHO ARE THEY...? OUR DADS...?
I...I CAN'T TELL...
WHY ARE THEY MOVING AROUND SO FAST? WE'LL NEVER CATCH UP AT THIS RATE....
I HAVE NO IDEA WHAT'S GOING ON...
HYOOOON
B-BM
BM

HF!
HF!
HF!
HF!
UNBELIEVABLE... I THOUGHT I TRAINED SO HARD IN THE AFTERLIFE... BUT WE'RE DEAD EVEN...
YOU MUST'VE TRAINED HARDER THAN I DID...
...NO...I THOUGHT I DID, BUT YOU'RE MORE GIFTED THAN ME...I COULD NEVER MAKE UP THE DIFFERENCE BETWEEN US...I FINALLY SAW THIS WHEN YOU FOUGHT BOBBIDI'S MONSTER...
...IT WAS A HUGE BLOW... THAT'S WHY I MADE UP MY MIND...

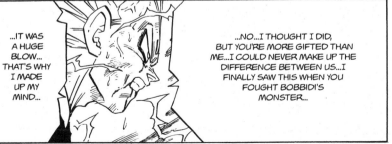

AT THE TOURNAMENT, THE GUYS WHO'D KNOWN BOBBIDI'S MINIONS MENTIONED THEY'D GOTTEN STRONGER...I THOUGHT... MAYBE IT WOULD CLOSE THE DIFFERENCE BETWEEN US... IF I LET HIM CONTROL ME...

YEAH...

YOU GOT BOBBIDI TO...

SO THAT'S IT...!!

...AND I WAS RIGHT...

...

YOUR PRIDE LET HIM CONTROL YOU...JUST TO GET STRONGER?

...

...THOUGH I HATED WHAT I HAD TO STOOP TO...

I...

I...

I GOT MYSELF A FAMILY... AND IT WASN'T SO AWFUL...I EVEN STARTED TO LIKE THE COMFORTABLE LIFE ON EARTH.

I HATED HOW YOUR INFLUENCE WAS MAKING ME SOFTER... LESS AGGRESSIVE.

I WANTED TO BE THE RUTHLESS AND COLD-BLOODED SAIYAN!! TO FIGHT IT OUT WITH YOU—NOT CARING ABOUT ANYTHING ELSE!!!!

I WANTED TO BE THE WAY I USED TO BE !!!!

• • •

...THAT'S WHY I NEEDED TO BE EVIL AGAIN...!

I FINALLY FEEL STRONG AGAIN!

THANKS TO BOBBIDI...

READ THIS WAY

To Be Continued In Dragon Ball Z Vol. 23!

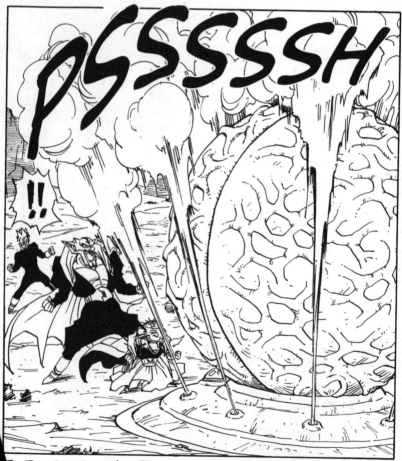

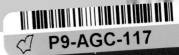

EXT VOLUME...

y djinn, Boo, has awakened! eign of terror begins, even izard Bobbidi and his allies whether such an uncontrol- g should have been set free. One by one, the universe's greatest champions are killed, crippled, or turned into candy...until finally, only one remains to put up a fight. Can Vegeta defeat Boo...and at what cost?! **AVAILABLE NOW!**